APRIL CALLS

by CHRIS MARSHALL

WANDERER PRESS
Published by
C.W. PUBLISHING

This book is based on actual
occurances. All personal names
except for mine, and all boat
names except for the Mary Day
have been changed.

C.M.

Copyright 1993 by Chris Marshall
All rights reserved
Cover design by Deron Graham
Photograph by Rachel Ganapoler

WANDERER PRESS
Published by
C.W. PUBLISHING
P.O. Box 695
Port Townsend, WA 98368

ISBN: 0-9637347-3-3

For Anne,
with love and appreciation.

...how singular, in the vastness of creation, is the richness of our opportunity.
John Cheever

ONE

April 30, 1992
Dawn

The sun piercing the horizon burst the silence of dawn and made the phone ring clamorously. With groggy reflexes I brought it to my ear and mumbled, "Hello." Slivers of sun embedded themselves in my eyes. I squinted, still half asleep, and repeated, "Hello?"

"Chris, is that you? It's April."

"April?"

The sun now shot arrows. They hit my pupils like bull's-eyes. It was April! I was wide awake. I switched ears and turned to see Autumn sound asleep beside me.

"April," I whispered with enthusiasm into the receiver, "where are you?"

"In the Caribbean, of course. Sorry, I know it's early there but I had to call to tell you that we're sailing for the Mediterranean after all."

"Who's we?" I asked.

"Steph and Joe and I. Steph is a friend of mine from from

Port Townsend. She lives down here now with a man named Joe on his sailboat the Island Girl, and I'm staying with them. We're leaving for Spain right after race week. No later than May 3rd. I know it's short notice, but you can come if you want."

It wasn't a dream. But still, like in a dream when you can't run or can't punch, I couldn't speak. My mouth was open and my mind reeling, but no words came. My eyes were full of pictures real and imagined of oceans and boats upon them, of the tropics and the high seas, but my mouth was empty of words. One finally surfaced.

"...maybe."

So much had changed since we talked about that trip. My part-time job was now full-time. My bare apartment was now cluttered. The woman I was dating was now a *relationship*. My life of travel and adventure had given way to domestic comforts. Had given way so far that though I was now being offered an opportunity I had dreamed about for years, I was not sure if I still wanted to take it. I had responsibilities to consider, priorities to access.

"Maybe?" she asked.

"Maybe," I replied.

There was a disappointed pause. "Well, O.K. You know how to reach me." The excitement that was in her voice a moment earlier now had nowhere to go. I wanted to yell something out to her, I wasn't sure what, but I held back and said, "O.K."

After a pause she said, "Well, this pay phone is costing me a fortune..."

"I'll let you know," I said.

She started to say something else, but we were disconnected.

The sun was just above the horizon when I hung up but in my heart it was high in the sky, and I was barefoot on a hot Caribbean beach. I reached down and scratched my feet. They were itchin' to go, and I knew that I must. The Siren song was in my ears. Wanderlust overtook my soul. Long ago I planted this trip in my mind and had fertilized it with years of dreams. Now that it was ripe I could no more deny its fruit, even if I had ceased to hunger for it, than I could deny my own breath.

Autumn slept in innocence, peaceful and unknowing. Sleep well dear friend for with waking comes betrayal.

TWO

May 10, 1992
4:00 AM

I steadied myself as the boat rolled over ocean swells and tried to stand up straight in a dark little room that was slanted at least forty degrees. Reaching into my pack I pulled out an unopened twelve-pack of Trojan condoms, "with special receptacle end." They weren't what I was looking for. The Dramamine seasick pills I was looking for came in a similar cardboard box except they were half gone. I swallowed one dry. I had five left. We had seven days to go, that should be enough. Just then my bunk mate burst in like someone who had been held underwater. He turned on the light, and I saw that he was soaked. Salt water dripped down his face as he said, "it's blowing like stink out there." Then, seeing my pills he asked, "You sick or something?"

"Just being prepared," I said. He mumbled something about the Boy Scouts and climbed under the covers of the bottom bunk without toweling off.

I noticed the label on the box of rubbers that said, "Don's Pharmacy," and for a second there I was not on my way up to a wave swept deck, rocked by the stormy Atlantic, going on watch at four a.m, but was walking comfortably down Water Street on a sunny spring afternoon in Port Townsend, Washington on my way to the pharmacy sunny with anticipation and optimism to buy a box of rubbers and some seasick pills. Be prepared! I threw both boxes back in my pack and pulled myself up through the narrow doorway. Preparedness, what a farce in terms of this trip. Who could be prepared for what I encountered, what I experienced, what I had just and was still living through? It would be like preparing for death. What do you bring along?

THREE

April 30, 1992
10:00 AM

I was going to bring along a nice French cabernet. I had laid in bed (staring wide-eyed at the ceiling like it was a massive genoa that had just come across the fore-deck and filled on a new tack putting me hard against the wind and oncoming swells) until the stores opened. My first stop was the pharmacy. From there I walked to the wine shop. As I walked I imagined a toast on deck. "To the sea," I'd say with a glass of the fine wine I so suavely pulled from my humble pack. They would reply in chorus, "To the sea!" But I was told at the wine shop that a bottle of wine costing forty dollars in Washington would sell for only fifteen dollars in the Caribbean, so I saved my money and planned on buying a fine vintage after I arrived.

From there I went to the bank and closed my account. Three thousand, one hundred and twelve dollars. It weighed heavy in my pocket like a gold brick. I took it to the travel agent and chipped a five hundred and fifty dollar chunk off of it in exchange for a one-way ticket to Antigua on American Airlines. Then I went to an antique shop in town and bought a one hundred dollar high quality used watch with a second hand which I reckoned I'd need while taking celestial navigation sights with the sextant.

Coffee was brewing when I got home. I put my bag on the table and poured myself a cup from the pot on the counter. Autumn came in wearing a robe and slippers. She kissed me and smiled. "What did you get?" she asked in complete ignorance as she stepped towards the bag. I didn't stop her. I couldn't think of how else to tell her. She was asleep when I left, and she was on the pill when she went to look into a bag of condoms. There was one last look of contentment on her face. One last moment when everything was as it should be and this was just another pleasant sunny morning. She opened the bag, and I watched clouds gray her face as her eyes and the corners of her mouth dropped. "What's this?" she asked, grasping for hope.

I spoke quietly. "I'm going to the Caribbean."

"When?"

I took a slow breath through my nose and said exhaling, "Tonight."

Her shoulders dropped as if weighted. She rushed softly to the bedroom and closed the door.

She had heard me talk about it, seen me read about it, knew I thought about it. Yet I don't think she ever thought I would really do it. Now, here it was like a stranger in strange dark clothes. An ugly thief she hoped would never arrive, yet now here it was. Unwanted, unwavering and right in her kitchen: my trip across the Atlantic.

FOUR

I can still remember the day, years ago. I had just come upon the answer to one question and that, of course, brought about another question.

The spirit of adventure lived in my heart and question, "Where does one go for adventure today?" was often in my head.

In the 1700's there was the new world, the Great Chance of America to which millions of people flocked. Children, convicts, fathers and mothers, young women and men stepping off into the unknown with vitality and daring.

In the 1800's there was the frontier. A day when Ohio was wilderness and Montana virtually unreachable from the east.

In 1849 there was the gold rush. A testimony to the longings for adventure which brewed in my heart is the fact that between 1849 and 1852 over 100,000 people made it to San Francisco either on foot across the continent, which was full of hostile Indians and deadly dysentery, or via the isthmus of

Panama which was disease infested and hard to get to and from -or, hardest of all, around treacherous Cape Horn and the worst seas in the world. Imagine Cape Horn without radar, satnav, or even a radio, aboard an old bark, or square-rigged clipper, or brig loaded to the gunwales with shovels, pickaxes, and young men yearning for adventure. Over 100,000 of them leaving their secure farms and familiar hometowns for a chance at handfuls of gold and the adventure of a lifetime. Returning, if they returned at all, sometimes richer, sometimes poorer, but always with a wealth of experience.

In the later 1800's there was the western frontier between the Mississippi and San Francisco. But even then Mark Twain thought of going to South America to find the adventure that was waning here. Instead he moved to Connecticut and wrote about his youth, "The Adventures of Huck Finn."

There was the forbidding north in the early 1900's -the Yukon of Jack London's stories. And in 1917 you could have all the adventure you wanted in the trenches of World War One.

Today there are McDonald's in Alaska, footprints all over Tierra Del Fuego, flags like pimples on all the tallest mountains of the world, trails crossing both poles like strings around a box, even tire tracks on the moon.

Again I ask, "Where does one go for adventure today?" To the intellectually inbred academic world of college? To the army to learn subservience and murder? On the road like Jack Keroac, dropping peyote and drinking beer wasted, and worn out between dingy old gas stations going nowhere? No.

My answer was, "For adventure today go to sea." There are no McDonald's at sea. If anything is unchanging it is the sea, if only because it is ever-changing. Eternal and churning with certitude, the same for me today as for my distant forefather sailing from Scotland so many years ago. I realized that true adventure must be somewhat contrived today. Gone are the days when one could take time off from college and sail from Boston to California as a deck hand like R.H. Dana as told in his book *Two Years Before the Mast*. A dozen ships a day sailed out of Boston in 1840. Ships that needed a hundred hands to operate them. You could sign on as a paid deck hand Monday night and leave Tuesday morning. Nobody pays you to sail today. Adventure of that kind costs money. Adventure was a part of life for our ancestors. Today it is a contrived commodity. It is adventure for adventure's sake not, as with the gold rush or Dana's sail to California, a natural part of one of life's potential endeavors.

I asked, and my answer was the sea. Granted, Antarctica today is no cake-walk, nor is there a Coke machine on K2. Adventure is surely to be had in those places. Others may have answered mountains, the desert, Central America, the Arctic, but for me the answer was, "Go to sea." And the obvious next question was, "How?" More specifically, I wanted to know how I could get on a boat sailing across the Atlantic Ocean.

I saw an ad for a trans-atlantic trip aboard a three masted ship called the "West Wind." I called them with my aforementioned visions of adventure in my eyes and the taste of salt air on my tongue. They said they would send me a brochure.

For two weeks I had boats swashing around my head and leviathans in my eyes. I was at the helm of a great square- rigger rolling over 30-foot swells and was reefing sails of thick wet canvas in a gusting storm as the Cutty Sark broke another record. I was not a little disappointed when I got the brochure. The "West Wind" was a one-thousand-foot-long (three-hundred meter) boat. A floating hotel. The sails were all computer controlled. The brochure actually said, "You won't have to worry about manning the decks and hoisting sails. You'll have plenty of time to man our lounges and hoist our expertly mixed drinks." Everyone but the employees looked over sixty five. Images of tying those reefing lines as sea spray drenched my face and penetrated my nor'westers, were replaced by images of fighting for the most cushiony chair at the morning geriatric alcoholics hoisting party, "Hi, I'm Misty, your expert mixologist." Needless to say, I saved my money.

After that I heard about schooner charters in Maine. I signed up for a week long stint aboard the Mary Day out of Camden. The sailing was enough to satisfy any purist. The boat was impeccable, the food incredible. But there were two major things wrong with that trip. First, we didn't go anywhere. We got on a boat in Camden and one week later we got off a boat in Camden. It was a round trip. We didn't even catch any fish. In that way, despite the authenticity of the vessel, the purity of the sailing, and the beauty of the scenery, it still felt somehow fake, contrived, like the Switzerland display at Disneyworld. No matter how rosy- cheeked the blonde who serves your "Swiss cocoa," you still know you're in Florida. It's a basic discrepancy which can't be covered up with fancy folk dancing or polished brightwork. Cruising Penobscot Bay on an old working schooner is like doing laps around a farm on an old tractor, but not plowing or planting seed. No matter how pleasant, it still seems somehow pointless.

Second, "due to insurance reasons" I wasn't allowed any of the best places. Guests were never allowed aloft (up in the rigging) and were not allowed on the bowsprit while the boat was under way, which is the best time to be there. With envious stares I'd watch the crew unfurl the topsails in light winds or stow the jib-topsail when the winds blew strong. They would sometimes stay aloft, standing on the upper spreaders keeping company with the topmast and enjoying what must have been a magnificent view, while I enjoyed the allowable "guest participation" which consisted of sheeting in, lowering the centerboard, or taking the helm for a few minutes in fair weather.

On the way back from Camden I stopped in Portland, Maine and had the good fortune to walk by the offices of *Ocean Navigator* magazine. I stepped in and asked the editor my question.

"If you want to sail across the Atlantic," he answered, "the place to be is in the Caribbean on the island of Antigua at the end of April. Every year at that time they have a thing called Race Week in English Harbour to commemorate the end of the winter charter season. The nicest boats from all the islands go to it and when it's over often need delivery crew to help bring them to the Mediterranean for the charter season in summer or to points all over the globe. In fact, that's how I first got across the Atlantic nearly fifteen years ago. And you can still do it today."

"How much sailing experience did you have at the time?"

"Just Lightnings around Lake Winnipesaukee."

That was all I needed to hear. Lightnings, a nineteen- foot

day-sailor on smooth Lake Winnipesaukee? I was a volunteer sailing instructor in Santana 22's on Monterey Bay. Sometimes even out into the Pacific Ocean! The seed of years of dreaming was thus planted.

For years the words "Race Week" rested on my horizon like a warm island in the distance, and every April I would hear the call and my mind would wander off to little English Harbour, as I wondered if the time was right. But there was always something. Either school or work or not enough money or another trip, but at the same time there was always the desire. That is, until I got to Port Townsend.

FIVE

April 30, 1992
11:00 AM

I stood in the kitchen until the steam stopped rising from my coffee before beginning to pack feverishly. There were three categories. The first and smallest was the stuff I was bringing. I once met a woman on a train who traveled with three big suitcases, a day-bag, and a full size sewing machine. She developed a great knack for finding nice people like me to help her carry them. On the other hand, I travel with only one small pack on my shoulder. I found my well-worn pack in the back of my closet and filled it with my road staples: a few clothes, toothbrush, razor, harmonica, one book to read and another to write in.

The second category consisted of things I wanted to keep. My typewriter and writings, my favorite books, nicer clothes, some letters and photographs. These went into a box to be mailed to my parents who by this time were used to receiving such packages, usually a day or two after I called and said, "Guess where I am now."

The third category was everything else, the stuff I was leaving behind, forgetting. It was a material desertion that some people couldn't imagine. For some, freeing themselves of material encumbrances and hitting the road may be a distant dream or a dreaded thought, but for others it is a common occurrence. Category three were the unimportant things. My eyes didn't even stop on them. My bed, dresser, couch, chairs and table, unessential books, a stereo, dishes and silverware, a blender. Who ever thought I would own a blender? Things I had acquired over the year I lived there I was now abandoning like jetsam. Except it wasn't the stuff that was getting jettisoned, it was me. I would get another bed, dresser, stereo, (blender?), more light reading, when I got to wherever I was going, just as I had acquired all that stuff here. Leaving on a journey is like a death, and I regarded all those superfluous possessions with as much value as would a dead man.

Whoever called it a travel bug was mistaken. The urge to roam is no sickness but a way of life, a basic necessity. It is the carbon molecule on which the whole of some peoples lives are based. It is a big dog on a thick leash dragging you wherever it wants to go. Onto planes, boats, halfway around the world, at the end of a short leash which you can't let go of. On the other end is an overgrown puppy of a sheep dog, his tongue hanging out as he doubles back and playfully knocks you down to lick your face. He runs off again with you trying frantically to keep up and laughing hysterically at the mad excitement of it all.

This may make it sound like a drug addiction or alcoholism, but that's not so. Alcohol is a pollutant. Travel is a purifier. Running water is the purest water, and stagnant water the most murky and alge infested.

But if the road is exciting and adventurous, it can also be lonely. And loneliness can be as blind as love. The room was in disarray when Autumn came back out of the bedroom. She still wore her robe and slippers. There was a shroud of silence about us as we moved around the room like strangers in a dance of distance. She was draped with sadness, and I could not comfort her. The one thing that would cheer her up was the one thing I couldn't do, and that was stay.

SIX

Port Townsend is where you get if you get to Seattle and keep going. If you're traveling for business or pleasure, you stay in Seattle. If travel to you means a round-trip ticket and a two-week stay, then go to Seattle. But if for you itchy feet is a permanent condition, if once you get to a place you immediately begin thinking where you can go next, then you end up in Port Townsend.

It is the end of the road, the top left corner of the United States, a refuge on the fringe, an extremity scattered with terminal moraine displaced from all over the world. It is Key West and Camden, Maine and the San Diego of Chuck Bukowski. Get drunk and lazy on a wooden boat, and enjoy the strange desolate scenery of isolation.

It was the first place I had ever been in my life that I felt I belonged and didn't think about where I wanted to go next a moment after I arrived. For the first time ever I got to a place and thought, "This is a place I could stay." New England and

Nebraska, nice places to grow up. Florida and California, nice places to visit. Port Townsend, nice place to live. This thought was wholly new to me, and I didn't know how to react to it. I took my apartment on a month-to-month basis. I took my job with the understanding that it would only be temporary. I met Autumn and told her early on that she couldn't count on me sticking around. At any moment I could be moving on. That's how it had been every other time I arrived somewhere. Except this time I had an unspeakable secret: I was thinking about staying. To admit this would be like Tipper Gore saying, "Gee, I kind of like some of those new thrash-metal bands." It was an urge so foreign to me that month after month I still told my landlady and my boss not to expect me to stay. I wasn't being purposely deceitful. I just didn't know how to act geographically stable. The words "six month lease" were to my mind what bacon is to a Muslim's tongue. They never even got far enough to be spit out. I thought I was rebelling to my new natural feelings, but in practice I was acquiescing completely.

I think it was a matter of concern between people who knew me. I'd say, "I may be quitting, or moving, or leaving next month," but day after day I'd be there, dependable as a drudge. They treated my talk of leaving like an innocent fantasy and allowed it as one allows children imaginary playmates. I was probably the only one to take my talk of leaving seriously, and that's only because I was too blind to see how domesticated I had become.

I already lived with Autumn when I met April. In her I saw a spark of recognition usually reserved for close family or movie stars. The immediate knowledge of, "That's someone I know." I knew her because in her I saw myself. It was like walking by a mirror in a department store when you don't expect it. You know yourself when you see you. It was the spark in her eye that I recognized, and I could tell by the way she looked at me that she saw it too, that we recognized each other as kindred spirits. When we talked her words could have been quotes from me. Talk of adventure and meaning and a life well spent. We were speaking each other's minds, and the recognition was amazing. I told her about my dream of sailing across the Atlantic and, what do you know? She had just bought a one-way ticket for the Caribbean, leaving in two weeks, would be there all winter, and would be in English Harbour in April! It was all too much to believe.

For those two weeks we met every day, for a coffee here, a lunch there. She was the personification of my spirit of adventure, and maybe it was because I felt it waning that I was so enticed by her. But it was more than that. It was my spirit of adventure calling me, taunting me, asking, "Will you listen?"

On the morning of the day she left, two weeks after we met, I noticed she was beautiful. I had been so busy seeing the me in her that I didn't even notice the her in her. "All this time and I never noticed how pretty you are," I told her. It was a revelation to me, to actually be able to spend two weeks with a beautiful woman and be interested only in her spirit, it was virtually unthinkable, but it came out sounding canned and insincere. I suddenly saw her in a new light. I could tell she sensed this, and our eyes met in a different way. But then the bus came and it was good-bye.

So many times I had been on the other side of teary-eyed

good-byes, with me being the one with the one-way ticket and my sweetheart being so sad to see me go, totally unable to grasp the wondrous fact that I was going to a great thing, an unknown adventure, going to the excitement and inspiration of confronting the unexpected on its own terms, that when April left I could feel nothing but the joy and excitement she felt. In that I was always so happy to be going, I was also happy to see her go. Then she was gone and I returned to my warm domicile for the winter.

Loneliness can be as blind as love. This is the pretext under which Autumn and I met and grew close. Our time together was a very pleasant one. We lived well together, ate well, made love often, and enjoyed each other's company. To all outward appearances it seemed ideal. Except for that small voice, that small spirit of change, of motion, of adventure that was dying, shriveling up like a raisin, and calling out to me. I would lay awake at night hearing it's cry. "What about me?" it would say, growing fainter and fainter, "What about me..." as Autumn slept peacefully beside me. In that darkness I felt I was being drained of my youth. In the light of morning we would wake up and make love. I was growing attached to her the way one does to family, a wife. Yet at the same time I was becoming torn and cloven of heart.

The tragic irony was that in arriving in Port Townsend I at once lost the desire to take this trip, while I also gained the opportunity.

All winter I wrote letters to April, one saying, "I'll be there next month," the next saying, "Leave without me, I'm not coming," and she wrote back telling me about the chartering world, dragging anchors, and Caribbean parties. My days were placid fields of contentedness and my nights tense labyrinths of indecision as I felt my youth dwindle, my gumption atrophy and the groove to my grave deepen.

But April called with a limited time offer. She was like a car dealer saying, "Sale ends tomorrow." The pressure was on. Take it or leave it. Life or death. Now or never. "Timing," said Jesus Christ, "is everything." What was I to do?

SEVEN

I went to the Uptown Pub for a bagel and a beer. A nicer place could hardly be imagined. Sunbeams poured through the windows, a cool breeze strolled through the open door, music played on the radio. The bartender played cribbage with two regulars at one end of the bar. I sat eating at the other. I could feel the plane ticket folded in my left pocket and the wad of bills in my right. I looked at my new watch like it was a star on the horizon. If I tried to think about my trip I came up with a blank. I was entering the unknown, on my way to a country I had only heard about, to a boat I had never seen, to sail across the Atlantic with three other people, two of whom I had never met. The only thing I knew about was April, and I had only known her for two weeks eight months ago. It wasn't a picture of her I had anyway, it was an idea, a way of life. When I thought of her I didn't think of brown hair or shining eyes, but of that spirit of spontaneity and motion, of an unquenchable lust for life.

The pub was empty but for the sun, the breeze, the cribbage players and myself. And the radio. It was a subtly blissful day full of bright skies and sunny horizons until the music stopped and the news entered. Something about riots in Los Angeles. "Seventeen dead...fires." I heard the phrase, "fearsome anarchy." Cribbage stopped, eating stopped, it seemed like even the breeze stopped. It wasn't as much the announcer's words that kept my ear glued as it was the background noise. He was reporting live, and in the background was the sound of death, of war, of hatred and fury. Death, of nineteen people before the broadcast was over, of our blissful ignorance and beautiful day so far away, and the implied death, in the way that sickness implies the death of a body, of the country as a whole. We sat there in silence even as the music started again. I thought to myself, "What a time to leave," not knowing if I meant a good time or a bad time.

When I got home Autumn was still in her bathrobe. She had been crying. I sat down on the couch beside her and put my hand on hers. She pulled away like from an electric shock. "Don't touch me!" she snapped. Then she leaned over and laying her head on my arm, cried softly. "I'm sorry," she said.

"What are *you* sorry for?"

"I'm sorry you feel you have to leave. It's O.K. if you want to split up. I can move out. You don't have to go all that way just because you don't like me." That's what she said. She took it personal. I tried to tell her that I wasn't leaving her but was going to something I had dreamt of doing for years. But semantics don't help heartaches and the facts were still the same. Whether I was leaving her or going to something else, she would still be alone in bed tonight and this made her sad. I put my arm around her, and she put her hand in mine. I asked, "What will you do?"

"Go back to Oregon, I guess. Move in with my sister or something. She could always use help with her baby."

"Why don't you stay here? You can take over the apartment, and you already know people."

She was crying slightly, "I can't stay here. Everyone I know is through you. I don't want to be here any more. I hate it here now." I stroked her head, and we sat for a long time without talking.

As I finished getting ready to go we weren't such strangers anymore. She was sad, and I was too excited for uncertainty. She sat on the couch as I ran frantically around the apartment, stopping to sit with her, together arm in arm as we had so many times. But comforting as I may have been, the six o-clock bus still had my name on it.

Everything packaged and mailed, I called work to tell them I wouldn't be in tomorrow, or the next day, etc. They weren't too happy about it, but pizza makers aren't that hard to find. They wished me well and asked when I'd be back.

"I don't know," I said. "I plan on sailing to the Mediterranean, then traveling around Spain for the summer. Hitchhiking in the mountains, learning some Spanish, checking out the Olympics and Worlds Fair. I was thinking I might be able to get some kind of job there picking olives, stomping grapes or selling gold medal souvineers."

"Sounds like quite a plan."

It sure did. The time had come. I kissed Autumn goodbye. We spoke a few words which barely made it out of our mouths before falling flat on the floor like soggy pancakes. As I closed the door behind me I heard her cry out loud.

EIGHT

April 30, 1992
9:00 PM

The last bus from Port Townsend got me to the airport three hours early. I entered the somnambulist ranks of airport dwellers and found a chair in front of a t.v. The death toll of the Los Angeles riots was at twenty-two by this time. The news seemed almost unreal in the antiseptic environment of the airport. A businessman talked on a cellular phone behind me, while someone on t.v. knocked down and jumped onto a phone booth. The reactions in the room seemed to range from incredulous nausea to complacent disinterest. Those from southern California voiced concerned paranoia. Those from elsewhere were silently glad that it wasn't happening where they were from.

I wished I had something meaningful to say on the subject, but as much as them I didn't know what to say or think. I was going far away from the problem and had other things on my mind. Or, more true, I had nothing on my mind. I was in a waiting daze in the airport's businesslike indifference.

The first leg of my flight went in the usual politely uncomfortable and informally uneventful manner of modern travel. I didn't meet anyone memorable or do or see anything memorable. I sat for three hours in an aluminum tube moving 600 miles an hour, and when I got out everything looked exactly the same; the red carpet and blue vinyl chairs of another American Airlines terminal. My ticket said Dallas, but the only thing that told me it was Dallas were the post cards.

I sat in a vinyl chair next to a woman with a plastic wig in polyester clothes. She was applying another coat of make-up with her right hand and drinking an artificially flavored, artificially colored orange soda, (sweetened with Nutri-Sweet), with her left. The only thing that wasn't artificial about her was her body bulging forth from elastic waist bands and her voice which squeaked out in a pudding-like falsetto untouchable by modern technology. "Hello," she said.

"Hello," I replied, only staring obliquely.

She slurped her drink empty and put away her make-up. "Just get here from Seattle?" she asked.

"Yes, and you?"

"We're on our way there now," she reached down to pick up her knitting, "to visit the kids. All the way from New Jersey."

She was knitting with orange polyester. "Who's that for?" I asked.

"This one's for me. It's going to be a sweater. I made one just like it for my husband. I like to make them a little snug to show off my knitting."

"I imagine he loves it."

"He sure does. And where are you going?"

"To the island of Antigua in the Caribbean."

"That's nice," she said absently as she knitted. "What will you do there?" she asked.

"From there I'll sail a boat across the Atlantic."

"Is that right?" she said without looking up from her knitting.

I noticed a stout man approaching in a tight orange knit polyester sweater. A blue and white striped rugby shirt showed clearly through the hexagonal holes. "Look at that beautiful sweater," I said to the woman. She looked up over her bifocals, and then at me.

"Why, thank you very much," she smiled.

He came up to us and said, "Why, Marge I can't leave you alone for a minute without some handsome young man trying to steal you away from me."

She chuckled, "Henry, this young man is going to the Caribbean to sail a boat to England."

"Spain, actually," I said.

"Well I'll be! How did you ever manage that?"

I told them about race week and how the charter season was in the winter in the Caribbean and in the summer in the Mediterranean, "and I've been invited to help bring a boat across."

"What's wrong with the Caribbean in the summer?" Henry asked.

"Hurricane season.

"Hmm."

"How about you?" I asked, "Looking forward to Seattle?"

"Oh yeah. We were there once before in '75. Great place,"

he said as he leaned back and put his hands on his belly as if remembering a dinner he had there. "Good food there I remember. Weather's not so good. Sure can't beat Jersey, but it's where our kids are so we go every so often."

Soon their flight was announced, and Henry and Marge said good-bye and headed for the boarding gate. As their matching polyester behinds faded into the crowd I felt strangely envious of their freedom from the endless desire to roam, envious for their ability to build their lives without that nasty travel stealing away months and years, envious that they could be satisfied with a trip to Seattle every seventeen years. I envied them until I realized that I never envied anyone like that before. The thought made me shudder. I shook it from my shoulders and ran for my next flight.

NINE

May 1, 1992
2:30 PM

Puerto Rico began as just another six hour airport layover. There were vacationing midwesterners on their way to cramming a year's worth of fun into two weeks and those on their way back looking vaguely dissatisfied and hung over. There were Puerto Rican families, big and natural even in the contrived airport environment, and businessmen walking around in hundred-degree weather in the internationally accepted three-piece business suit/wake wear. And there was me, looking like a cross between a teenage runaway, a drug smuggler, and a graduate student scribbling away at my thesis in letters to friends.

What happened next I can neither ease into nor romanticize; I lost all my money in a Puerto Rican casino. It wasn't even all that eventful. I had six hours to kill so I took an airport van to a local hotel with a casino. People there drove like nuts. It was as if they all woke up that morning and found the place full of cars so they jumped in them and tried to drive. Rudolf Valentino passed on the right at 95 mph. Latin lovers should be confined to galloping steeds, I thought, lest the strength of their passion cause a ten car pile-up.

I arrived at the casino where they very politely and very efficiently took all my money. I lost in thirty dazed minutes what it took me all winter to save. Two and a half thousand dollars gone in the blink of an eye and nobody even noticed. No crowds formed, no glamorous women hung on my arms as the chips piled high in front of me like buildings until the final throw of the dice, the double or nothing, the do or die. There was no hushed expectation as I shook them bones and blew on my hands for luck, letting them roll with a casual flair and confident smile... It wasn't anything like that. My wad of bills, my financial reservoir flowed in a steady stream from my hands into slot machines and black jack dealers' banks until my pockets were empty, my well run dry. Just then two people walked by. One asked the other, "Feel lucky?" Up until I lost my second to last chip I had felt lucky, like next time, next time, next time, the tides would turn, and I would start raking it in. I repeatedly walked back and forth from the tables to the chip window "feeling lucky." But a casino isn't a tidal pool it's a toilet bowl, flush flush, there goes all your money, there's no tide to change, just a clean white bottomless bowl waiting for you every time.

I stood lost and in shock with my hands in empty pockets, surrounded by the extra-gaudy island charm motif which had previously suggested to me how much money they had to lose, but now showed me how much money they had taken from dupes like me. A friendly waitress came up to me and asked if

I would like a free drink. I ordered a double pia colada. It came back in a large curved glass with an umbrella and a straw. Women in sequined evening gowns walked by with men in Hawaiian shirts and Bermuda shorts. Dapper gentlemen in tuxedos strolled around surveying the scene knowingly. I sipped that silly drink in jeans and sneakers, standing with the straw in my mouth like a pacifier as incredible amounts of money passed before my eyes like ex-girlfriends with new lovers saying, "You can look but don't touch." I had felt lucky. Now all I felt was the gambling hangover of stupidity. I felt physically sick, and sick at heart, and sick in a deranged sort of way like there was something very wrong with me that I would do this to myself. Though all providence was not lost. I did save one five dollar chip which I exchanged with great care next to a man turning in a handful of five hundred dollar chips like they were nothing. Added to the money I had in my pocket, that made exactly five dollars and fifty cents.

I got into a cab heading back to the airport and leveled with the driver. I told him I lost all my "dinero" in the casino and had only five dollars. Either out of compassion or gratitude for my economic support of his pueblo, he took me to the airport, an eight dollar ride, for only four dollars.

As amazing as it may seem, there was a part of me that cheered at that moment. That moment I was ultimately wise and ultimately foolish. I felt a freedom from the burden of money. I was myself and only myself. Cleansed in a way. It was a clear-headed feeling, like waking up well after a long sickness, cool after the fever has passed. I got on the plane to Antigua as one against the world. Forging ahead come what may, facing the ultimate challenge using only my cunning and wits. A globe trotting Huck Finn laughing in the face of adversity. David Copperfield on the road, the pauper adventurer. I'd live on salt air and cultural diversity, savoring the richness of mankind and sauntering around the globe as a brother and friend to all...

Antigua immigrations did not agree.

TEN

May 1, 1992
11:30 PM

When I arrived in Antigua it was dark and still 100 degrees. The airport was one runway, a chain link fence and a small building. In the building were three immigration booths, each with its own line. They moved slowly and steadily with the traffic of vacationing foreigners in pastels and white leather bags, and inter-island traffic in work clothes and duffel bags. Then came my turn.

The immigrations woman looked at my passport, then asked to see my ticket to leave.

"I'm leaving on a boat," I said with hintings of pride.

"Is the captain here to meet you?" she asked.

I had planned on surprising them. My image of English Harbour was such that I imagined I could get there and actually swim out to the boat, climb aboard and say, "Surprise!" I thought the water was warm and the people beautiful, and that I'd be spontaneous and romantic. But the surprise was on me. No one knew I was coming. No one was there to meet me. "He's waiting for me on the boat." I said.

Then the indignation began, "You have to buy a ticket out if you want to stay in the country. How much money do you have.?"

I exaggerated, "Two dollars."

"Two dollars!" she yelled and turned to the other women in their booths. Waving my passport she said, "Dis boy tryin to come here with jus two dolla's!" That's when my line stopped and the others stopped as the people looked on like rubberneckers at a car accident.

I saw some humor in it until the scorn in their eyes hit me. She turned and spat, "Bloody 'merican." There my misconceptions of a loving world community quickly evaporated. Their hate for me was obvious. I was not me but every rich obnoxious tourist they had ever dealt with, and their indignation was unrelenting. I no longer represented economic support and so was not spoken to with condescending politeness but blatant hatred. With vengeful eyes she asked again, "Where is the captain of dis boat?"

"He's waiting for me on the boat." I repeated.

"That is not good enough, boy. You go sit on that bench right there." She stamped my virgin passport with big blue words, "REJECTED," put it in a the top drawer of her desk, and pointed to the bench as if to a dog. That quickly, my vacation was over.

There was no questioning her. I went and sat on the long wooden bench next to the office with my pack by my feet. It was the grade school principal's office all over again except this time I was really in trouble. And there was another eerie twist.

The door to the office was open, and there was a radio playing reggae music and the news of the L.A. riots with a clear journalistic slant saying things like, "Our brothers and sisters are really rippin' it up in California." The immigrations people cheered, "All right mon," at the news of burning police cars and looted stores. "Go, baby," they would say like fans at a football game. I had flown five thousand miles away from Los Angeles and landed right in the middle of the riots. I had seen enough of the t.v. reports and of the morning paper in Texas to know as I sat on that bench that I was the enemy. I was the blue-eyed devil, the oppressor, the hated Man. Me, with a dollar fifty in my pocket and a harmonica in my pack, I was the evil one. The radio reported race riots in Los Angeles, Washington D.C, New York, Atlanta, Georgia, but they missed the little one in the airport at St. Johns, Antigua of which I was to be the only victim.

The people in the lines before me dispersed like zoo goers until only the keepers and I were left. There were four of them, three women from the booths and an overseeing man. Their faces were very dark and had potential for warmth, but to me they gave only grimaces and scorn. Their black eyes were like cold coal as they stood in front of me like a firing line and shot me full of holes with their hatred. "Who do you think you are, boy?" one said. "Dis is not a charity country!" another said. "We'll take care of you good!" they said as if speaking from one mind. "We gonna give you over to the police. They take care of you real good." They scathed me with their hate, while in the background Bob Marley sang on the radio, "One love, one love, lets get together and feel all right."

The three women had identical bodies. Their thighs were

as big as my waist, and their asses were like two large pillows full of craters and wrinkles like some comic image of obesity. I imagined them, three fit youths getting their jobs together, working together, eating together and going home in similar cars to similar homes, so that their bodies blew up to be three bulging replicas. The man was younger than them, thin and athletic, and stood an inch taller than me at 6'3". I looked to him for a sort of glimpse of affinity. We were about the same age and I hoped for a look of familiarity that would align us, but there was none. He looked straight ahead, and if I moved straight ahead he averted his gaze. The women were obviously in control, and they continued to riddle me with accusations and blunt rhetorical questions.

There was a telephone directly in front of me with a marine radio right next to it. I had a number for the boat and could have cleared it all up with just one phone call. I asked to use it.

"Do not touch that phone, boy," they said, threateningly.

"If I could just call the captain on the marine radio..." I began to say.

"Hey boy," they said, pointing at me, "we are not your family. It is not our job to take care of you. You should've thought of that," they spoke slow and condensingly, "a long time ago."

From down their noses I felt the evil stare and heard the words, "You cannot enter dis country without a ticket to leave unless the captain of your vessel is present to sign you on to the crew list." Their pleasure was evident as they told me, "You are a refugee now, boy."

"So, what happens now?" I asked.

"You just sit here and wait. We'll take care of you soon enough." They started to sift away. One of them brushed against my knee and repeated menacingly, "We'll take care of you good, blond-y," whatever that meant. I felt like she wanted me to react so she could further vent her hatred and exercise her little station of control, but I didn't give her the opportunity. They had the noose of bureaucracy around my neck, and there was nothing I could do.

For the next two hours I got to sit there wondering what they meant by, "take care of you good," as the radio played "Chant Down Babylon," and news of the riots.

The women would shuffle by lethargically in the heavy evening heat, being sure to look down at me despisingly each time as if it were their duty. If I laid sideways on the bench they'd say, "Hey boy, no layin' down on de job." I smiled politely to one woman as she passed by, trying to keep things light, but there's no such thing as an infectious smile in such a situation. "You smilin' or grinnin' at me, boy?" she said, as if grinning were the same as flipping her the bird.

"Smiling," I said.

"You better not be grinnin' at me."

They listened to the news from L.A. with distinct interest and cheers, saying,"All right," or "That's the way," in response to the violence and destruction. There were twenty-seven known dead by this time, more injured, fires and looting. That was all they talked about. When talking to me, their "refugee" as they called me, they continuously mentioned the police. At the end of my time with them I was to be "taken care of" by the local cops until I could be kicked out of the country on the first plane in the morning.

Somewhere in my memory was the phrase, "like a crushed pomegranate with teeth," pertaining to a guy getting beat to shit in some small African country. That was all I could think about when they mentioned the police. Inside I felt like groveling and pleading, "But I'm a pacifist. I read Albert Schweitzer!" but on the outside I remained surprisingly cool and restrained. If I was to be beat to shit like some rotten-toothed pomegranate I would accept that fate with stoic resignation. That was how I felt as my friends at the immigration service went about their business shuffling their feet as they brought paperwork back and forth across the room, trying unsuccessfully to antagonize me. I sat not feeling particularly comfortable or uncomfortable, just knowing that I wasn't beat to shit yet and that that was good.

ELEVEN

May 2, 1992
1:30 AM

You are a refugee now. It doesn't matter what kind of family you came from or how popular you were in high school, nor how much money you once had. It doesn't matter if just four days ago you were sitting in the comfortable shade of the Town Tavern sipping cold ale watchging the sun stream in bright and strong through the big side windows giving the pool balls oval rolling shadows, and a pretty tourist walked by and smiled right at you. That doesn't matter, nor does anything you once were, nor anything that once was. You are a refugee now, you are in custody, and nothing that was matters anymore.

The radio announced again twenty-seven dead and I saw myself an the potential number twenty-eight. The video tape I had seen on tv now played in my head with the colors reversed; it was black cops surrounding a white guy, kicking and clubbing him hard. That white guy was me. I was consoled by the fact that Antigua police probably didn't have stun guns. My friends in immigrations tried so hard to impart in me a fear of their police that when I saw them coming and they were not masked marauders with whips and chains, chain mail, flak jackets, AK-47's and fangs, I was considerably relieved.

I was thinking, "If the immigration personnel are this angry and mean, then what can I expect from the police?" But the police officer who came for me gave no clues as to what terrors awaited me back at the station. He was silent and professional and blasted reggae music for the whole drive.

The station was a two-story brown brick building. No other buildings were in sight. I saw sodomy and brutality and every horrible prison scene I had ever heard of when I looked at that building. The only light in the vicinity was that which came from the lobby. I was led up five bare stairs to the sergeant who sat at the front desk. Without looking up at me he spoke the words, "Here for?"

"Immigration purposes," my escort answered.

The sergeant's head rose slowly as he finished what he was reading. He looked me up and down. I awaited scorn and hatred, bodings of pain, a look promising violence. His eyes hit my clothes and my bag and ultimately, my eyes. According to him, I thought as I saw his reaction, there are two kinds of people: us and them, law enforcers and law breakers, criminals and non-criminals. He saw me at once as a non-criminal and treated me accordingly. He said with efficient unconcern bordering on sympathy, "Show him to the bed," and looked back down at his paperwork. I couldn't believe it. They were actually being nice to me! I took an immediate liking to him for not wanting me beat to shit. Considering the change in attitudes, I explained to him my circumstances and that there was a boat waiting for me if I may use the phone for just one short call...?

He replied, "You can stay here until we return you to the custody of immigrations in the morning. You may not use the phone." But at least he was nice about it, and I was grateful to him for that. That was before I saw the bed.

They too knew about the L.A. riots. They asked me about them, the death and the violence, but it seemed to me that they saw too few white people to generalize me into a hated enemy. The immigrations people could be full of hate because they saw me as just another rich foreigner, so much like every other rich foreigner that they didn't bother to really look at me. I was a "them" as far as they were concerned. Just another fat and happy American. But to the cops I was not a them, but me. They had no preconceptions or prejudices to blind them. For them I was not preceded by two hundred thousand tourists a year. To them I was a person, not a stereotype or a statistic, but an individual.

I was shown to a single bed under a staircase beside the lobby. There was a mattress and either a sheet or a thin blanket, depending on if you laid down beneath it or on top of it. It didn't really matter which as it looked about as clean as the mattress which looked about as clean as the floor which didn't look clean at all. I know nothing of the living conditions for the locals on the island, but this was considered a fine room.

Too much was on my mind to even feel drowsy. I spent the night sweating, slapping mosquitoes, and worrying about my well being. Nothing threatening actually happened, but every new person into the station had to pass by the stairwell to look at me. I was just a curiosity, but my small pack was now all I had and I felt I had to watch it closely. Who do you report it to if the police rip you off?

I had the pleasure of imagining all the bacteria, fungi, and various body lice that were making me their new home as I laid there awake with a reticent hunger that was eclipsed by my thirst that was greatly magnified by the fact that I didn't know if the water there was safe to drink. But those discomforts of the body were inconsequential compared to what was on my mind. It suddenly became clear to me all I had thrown away, and I missed it terribly. I had a sunny apartment, money in the bank, a clean, comfortable bed, a job, friends, a refrigerator full of food, and Autumn, oh Autumn, what had I done to her? Not only had I ruined my own life, but I had taken her with me. I knew the extent of her emotional dependence on me, an emotional dependence I helped develop and had disregarded entirely. I was lonely and remorseful beyond description. Had I just stayed in Port Townsend I'd now be sleeping contentedly beside an equally contented woman. But instead we were both miserable. She feeling rejected and I alone amidst strangers in an unkind land. I really blew it. It was nobodies fault but mine. I now had neither the comforts of home and Autumn nor the excitement of April. I had jumped for it and come up short. "What have I done?" I asked my palms pressed against my face. What had I done to myself and to this woman I cared for? I was mourning for her as for a dead person, and for us, and for my emotional framework which had been crushed.

At about three I went to the bathroom. The police jumped when I came out of the room. They had known I was there, but still I was a surprising spectacle. A non-criminal in custody, and a white man in a largely black world. Not wanting to end up hanging from my feet getting whipped for leaving my room without permission, I asked if it was O.K. for me to use the bathroom. They said it was, "No problem, mon." They related to me not as the enemy or criminal but as someone being sent home, and treated me accordingly. I was a curiosity but not an adversary.

I had to go back to my little room because, apparently, they had no word in their language for toilet paper so it was a good thing the Joseph Conrad book I had brought along was a used paperback, old and soft. I pulled off the last twenty pages and left some for them to read.

It poured rain at about four a.m. The rain fell like a weak metaphor of my sorrow. Tears of death and birth wetting the world around me and deepening the tepid puddles of self-pity in which I was wallowing. It poured for about twenty minutes, then stopped as suddenly as it started, though my remorse remained.

Morning came not as a relief nor a burden. It was just there after a while. It came with the sounds of wind rustling big tropical leaves and the calls of exotic birds ringing in my ears with distinct unrecognition. I hadn't slept one minute. I got up and walked out into the lobby of the building. The same sergeant sat at the desk with a thin teenager beside him. I asked if I could sit out on the front steps and he said it was O.K.

I sat on the front steps of the police station waiting for the sun to rise in the opaque grays of incarceration. The clouds were high misty slates, cold and encapsulating, wan in the pre-dawn light. Burn off as they may as the sun rose higher, I was still detained, thwarted, a kept charge.

The air was fresh but humid, and in the morning silence I could hear the Sergeant talking to a young man who had been brought in during the night for stealing.

"...You've got to ask yourself," he said, stern and fatherly, "what kind of man do you want to be? Do you want to be the kind of man that steals and robs, that does things like this? Because that kind of man ends up in this place behind the bars behind those doors." I could almost hear the young man's nods. "Or do you want to be another kind of man, the kind of man that is out there in the world doing something, being somebody. You are going to be a man soon and you must ask yourself, what kind of man do you want to be?" He spoke in the slow resonant way of island people, deep and mellifluous. His voice was the only thing in the in the still morning air of the station, and it hung there like palm leaves swaying on a breath as the sky cleared and brightened in tiny increments, moving towards dawn like the hour hand of a clock. He added after a pause, "...It is all up to you."

TWELVE

May 2, 1992
6:30 AM

When my friend from immigrations arrived he was as friendly as if he too had not slept a wink and was as witty a conversationalist as you may find in the rows of your garden. The police waved good-bye as we drove drearily away. It was like we were in the antisocial co-workers carpool. We drove silently through the weary and humid haze and arrived at the airport with the earliest of birds. I wished he would just drop me off, but as it turned out we worked in the same department.

I was to be deported, extradited, kicked out of the country to the nearest U.S. port which, as far as they were concerned, was San Juan, Puerto Rico.

We got in line at the outdoor ticket counter to talk to the American Airlines woman about getting me on a plane. I tried to get him to reason. I told him that if they were going to fly me out anyway, then why not just let me in as if I actually had a ticket. If I couldn't get on a boat I'd come back and let them kick me out then. But he didn't go for it. I asked again about using the phone or the marine radio but he said it wasn't his job to answer questions, it was his job to get me on the plane. I was dealing with every stupid petty bureaucrat I had ever dealt with. I was saying, "But officer, I was only going forty," just in another language and in more serious circumstances. I said, "Just think for one second," but thinking wasn't a part of his job. Get him to think and he's working overtime. His pay doesn't cover it, and he feels like he's getting ripped off. His world was a square hole and I was a round peg about to be mindlessly thrown out of the game. His was a small position of power, but he was going to exercise it to its full extent. My attempts at convincing him soon became redundant in the face of a faceless cog and I stood silently in line, thinking of what my life was to become.

I would get deported to Puerto Rico, the "rich port," virtually penniless, and would have to choose between entering the Salvation Army line or, at the age of twenty-five, calling my parents to bail me out. They would, of course, and I would move into their home in the sterile southern California suburb where they now live and dig myself out, spoonful by sorry spoonful, from under the cold tombstone of "I told you so." Those words would never be spoken. They wouldn't have to be. Every bit of advice I never took, about finishing college, staying with a job, spending my money on lasting material things instead of travel and the fleeting muse of experience, would echo in the halls of failure and defeat. I had always lived my life my way and now, the unspoken admonishment would ring, look where it had gotten me.

I wished I could just be back in bed with Autumn, stroking

her hair and caring for her. Oh, the comfortable life I gave up, the hurt I brought to her and I. "What have I done," I silently asked myself, "Why didn't I just stay. How contented we were. Why couldn't I have been satisfied with good enough?" How I wished I could be back there with us leaning on each other. Neither one of us would be sad. We would both be happy enough. It was co-dependancy at the airport keeping me leaning towards the past.

We arrived at the desk. The American Airlines woman there was the rudest person I encountered on the whole trip. The fact that I came to her in the custody of an immigrations officer meant that I was a piece of shit in her eyes. She was in the same American Airlines uniform I had been seeing for days, but she hit me with a level of hatred and disdain I had never seen before or since. "What is wrong with you? Get the fuck off our island, boy. Get the fuck out our country," she said with sharp daggers in her voice. Her eyes were black and vacuous. I looked away. I couldn't escape her words but at least my eyes could rest on something more pleasant. I looked off at some clouds rising above the center of the island and then at some people arriving in cabs. The plane was to leave in an hour, and the paying customers were beginning to arrive. Attractive Europeans with San Tropez tans and aloof expressions got in the line behind me. A man in a Panama hat got out of a limousine. The woman said, "Look at me when I'm talkin' to you, boy." I saw April paying for a ticket two lines down.

April! Was it really April? She was tanner and her hair was different, but it was April getting out of that line! I left my captor, telling him over my shoulder as I walked towards her that she was one of the crew on the boat. He tailed me like an angry shadow grabbing at me as I walked away.

"April," I called to her from behind, not really believing that it was her.

She turned to me, "Chris?" She couldn't believe it was me either.

"I just got here," I said.

"I'm just leaving," was her reply.

There were many things to say next, considerate, social things like, "Glad to see you," or "You look good," but before I could stop them the words came out of my mouth, "Loan me two hundred and fifty dollars."

"What are you talking about?"

I explained that I was about to be deported, and that the only way I could stay in the country was if I bought a ticket out.

She asked, "Didn't you bring any money?"

I could have easily lied. I could have said I had been ripped off or pick-pocketed in Puerto Rico. I could've said I lost the money and would not have looked like as much of a fool, but I could not. She was the beauty and truth in the face of which I couldn't lie.

"I did. But I lost it all in a casino."

"Oh Chris," she said in a disappointed motherly way, "how could you?"

I shrugged without words.

She had worked on a charter boat all winter and had made a lot of money. She matter-of-factly reached into her purse and supplied me with the travelers checks. I handed them over in exchange for a one-way ticket to San Juan, Puerto Rico.

How I wanted to taunt my ex-friend in the immigrations service as he was forced by the mighty regulations he had been upholding all morning to let me go, to slip from his grasp, to escape into the wilds of his country. I wanted to stick out my tongue and wave my hands with my thumbs in my ears but I I felt the power of his authority too strong to attempt too much impudence and decided not to take my chances. I also wanted to shake his hand and pat him on the back in thanks for the part he played in this drama, but the desire to just get the hell away from that airport was by far the strongest.

We walked over to the cab she had just gotten out of.

"I thought I would surprise you," I said with a smile.

"Surprise," she smiled back and looked into my eyes. "I decided to leave just this morning."

"Spur of the moment," we quietly said together.

I asked, "how did you get here with just a one-way ticket?"

"I didn't fly into Antigua. I flew into the U.S. Virgin Islands. You don't need a round-trip ticket to get in there because it's part of the U.S. Then I sailed here on the boat I was working on."

"Where are you going now?"

She looked at me and hesitated. "Back to California to stay with my parents for awhile, I guess. I don't know, I just woke up this morning and felt I shouldn't go to Europe. Something about it didn't feel right. And," she paused strangely, "and I haven't seen them in so long..."

To stay or to go, it was an indecision I could understand.

"How about you, will you still make the crossing with Joe and Steph?" she asked.

"That's what I came here for. I'm not going to come all this way just to turn back. And Barcelona is the place to be in ninety-two."

Somehow we were holding hands though I don't remember reaching out to hers or her taking mine. We were standing very close. I closed my eyes and could feel her near me. It wasn't a smell or a sound but another sense. Did I sense she felt it too? I could've gotten on the plane with her that morning and convinced my parents to charge me a ticket from Puerto Rico. I could've gone with her all the way back to California, and I imagined doing so. But I had not come to kindle a romance. I had come to live a dream. To have an adventure, not an affair.

"It sounds great," she said. I agreed.

There was a moment of awkward silence just before they announced her flight. We hugged and departed with the quick efficiency of people for whom departures are a routine part of their lives.

I got in the cab and said , "English Harbour."

"You know that woman, eh?" the driver said as we drove away.

Yes, I thought, very well.

THIRTEEN

May 2, 1992
8:00 AM

I was immediately suspicious of the cab driver. Who was this man and where was he taking me? We were driving down a back road. Where was the highway between the airport and English Harbour? Why weren't there any signs? He wasn't that big. I figured if he tried to pull over to beat me up and steal my stuff, I could probably take him. But what if he drove me to a house full of toughs? He probably thought I had a bunch of money. I wouldn't have a chance. I'd be beat up and left for dead in some back road ditch, never heard from again. Or else I'd crawl half naked back to that same police station where they would be enraged at my ingratitude, "We give you the most comfortable bed in the house and you crawl back to us looking like this?" and pummel me incessantly. I eyed the cab driver once more with thoughts of wrestling the wheel from him, pushing him out the door and driving off on my own.

A sleepless night of incarceration, when you lose all control over your welfare and are at the mercy of those in charge of you, who may or may not be very merciful, can make one rather paranoid. It's like waking up in a morgue surrounded by dead people. You can never see living the same again.

The landscape was like Ireland with low rocky hills, except much dryer. I had been to Ireland once many years ago. I remembered the young innocent I was when I was there, and then I remembered that there are no highways in Ireland, and few signposts. Even the houses and little towns we passed through were similar to Ireland, except here everyone was black. I was consoled by this, and it helped me regain my senses, only retaining a little of my suspicion. I asked the driver to stop at a roadside fruit stand. I got out and bought us each a juicy mango.

In the same way that I had expected a highway, I also had a picture in my mind of English Harbour that was like all the other harbors I had been to. I was imagining Shilshole marina in Seattle, the Santa Barbara harbor, and Mystic, Connecticut; places that have more parking spaces for cars than slips for boats. We came to a few small wooden buildings and a small bay full of boats. The driver stopped at the beginning of a dirt road. "This is English Harbour," he said. I felt like saying, "Are you sure this is English Harbour?"

My plane ticket came to $233.00. The cab ride would normally cost eighteen dollars, but since I bought him a mango he gave it to me for sixteen. The mangos were fifty cents for both. All told, I now lived up to my previous exaggeration and had exactly two dollars.

It was the Saturday morning after the Caribbean's biggest party of the year, and there weren't many people up. I shouldered my pack and began walking down the road where I was dropped off. Two men walked by me and one rubbed his chin saying, "This looks like a nice place. It's the first time I've seen it sober."

At the end of the road was a small bungalow-style hotel. There was a water hose beside it, and I drank from it with a ten-hours-of-sweating thirst. With my mango in hand, I went out to the beach to watch the harbor awake. The water was calm and the sand cool beneath me. Not a dingy disturbed the silence that early. I had not eaten since Texas. I peeled the succulent fruit and savored it with an appreciation reserved for the really hungry. The image of the starving man crawling in from the desert and ravenously devouring a plate of food was created by someone who had never experienced true hunger. When you're really hungry, food becomes a precious thing to your tongue. The mango tasted like a new creation, a sweet luscious bounty of the earth, and I ate it with deep appreciation, each bite revealing nuances of flavor I scarcely thought imaginable. I let them sit on my tongue like a connoisseur of the fruit.

As I sat on that beach I thought of how I was now nothing. I was not a student or employee or tenant or boyfriend. I was not a father or spouse. I wasn't on any roster or list. I had no connections, was unaffiliated, an independent. No one was waiting for me or looking for me. I wasn't even a refugee any more. Nor was I a son or brother, those things becoming distant abstractions at such a time. I was as good as dead. Or, more true, like a newborn baby. I was an infant on my own without parents or friends to take care of me, or position or possessions to support me. I was a premature baby, so anxious to get going in this world that I almost killed myself by getting here before I was ready. All I was, everything about me was sitting there on the beach. What you see is what you get. I had me, my clothes, a small pack, and the pungent sweet taste of mango slowly fading from my tongue. Absolutely nothing more. Just me, sitting on the shore feeling a few feet away from where life and death meet.

One sees through different eyes at times like these, with newness and clarity. Like a child, only more-so because it is greater to see as a child, to have the filters and learned precognitions of adulthood removed after one is already an adult. It carves the feelings, sights, sounds and smells clearly into your mind.

In a way, I wasn't even on the trip anymore. All I wanted was the past back, and in that way I was among the living dead. I was not on the trip I had dreamed about for so many years, but was on my way backwards to my future. My adventure was over. I was now on a journey of reconstruction.

Soon a few people motored in quietly. The place was waking up. I laid back on the sand and saw that above me on the balcony of the hotel was a couple having breakfast. They were naked. They were not interesting, intriguing or sexy or anything to me except threatening or unthreatening. My state of mind was such that I felt my freedom could be taken away at any time like a simple possession. Like an ex-con just out, I felt like my life was still on the verge of being re-confiscated. But those naked people didn't have anywhere to put handcuffs so they were O.K. They didn't seem to mind my presence, but I got up and walked away anyway.

That morning became the standard by which I judge all bad situations, the measuring stick of shitty circumstances. Being late on your car payment is one thing. Being broke with a paycheck on the way is one thing. Having only other people's money to spend is one thing. Having to wonder which friend's house you can go to for dinner is one thing. Having two dollars at dawn in an expensive foreign country where a fried egg costs two-fifty, not a familiar face for four thousand miles in any direction, and no way to get from that spot except to an equally bad spot -that's another thing all together. Just for having good water and not being a deportee, I was happy.

I walked back down the same dirt road on which I had arrived. I found the yacht club which consisted mainly of a bar and an upstairs I never saw. People were drinking already and talking about how drunk they got the night, or whole week, before. I asked for a glass of water. I was quite thirsty but couldn't afford the luxury of hunger.

I was wrong. I had more than just my few possessions. I had a past which enabled me to fit in unnoticed. It doesn't really matter if you don't have any money as long as you don't look like you don't have any money. I put on an aristocratic expression of benign complacency and was treated just fine. Though I felt like an empty store front on a Hollywood set, a facade with nothing behind it. My hair was trimmed, if disheveled, and I had a one day beard, but that wasn't uncommon there. My clothes were clean and not cheap. In short, I didn't look anything like the destitute, transient, homeless bum that I now was. Though I had lost a great deal of self-respect and felt my very personal dignity threatened, I was treated pretty much the same as the old me. Though I felt if anyone looked too closely into my eyes they would see my emptiness clearly. I felt like my future lay in being "that bum in the Izod shirt," but at the moment I was O.K, resting on what few laurels I had. It's a strange thing to see yourself only as a reaction in other people. Your only mirror being other people's faces. Am I, as that American Airlines woman at the airport seemed to think, just a piece of shit or, as the crowd at the yacht club treated me, an acceptable part of society? Had I not already had a viable self-image, had I in fact been an infant and been developing from scratch an image of myself, I would've been in big trouble.

FOURTEEN

May 2, 1992
10:30 AM

Every bar in English Harbour has a marine radio. I felt I was stretching the limits of my acceptability when I asked to use the yacht club radio, but they didn't react adversely.

On channel 68 I said, "Island Girl, Island Girl, Island Girl; yacht club," as it is the etiquette there to say who you are calling three times, then where you are calling from once. I repeated my call but got no reply.

My worse case scenario (fly to Puerto Rico with my ticket, get bailed out by my parents from there, move back into their house like a lost puppy, and get a wretched job at Dunkin' Donuts baking krullers and putting my life back together, both from scratch) was already mapped out. Most anything else looked better. I asked for another glass of water, this time egregiously requesting ice and a lemon. I got it all.

Steph had left Port Townsend before I arrived, but we knew some of the same people. She lived with Joe on his boat. Joe and I were complete strangers. After awhile I called again,

57

and Steph answered the radio.

"Island Girl, yacht club, switch to channel 60," was what she said.

"Hi, Steph? This is Chris, April's friend." I said hesitantly.

She reacted with unbelievable enthusiasm. "Oh my God, I don't believe it!" she said laughing. "We were just on our way in. Meet us on the end of the yacht club dock."

That was easy enough. I walked out to the end of the dock. Antigua during race week is literally full of the nicest boats in the world. Take the most impressive boat out of any marina in the United States and bring it to Antigua for race week, and it will be average at best. Boats I had actually seen in the pages of sailing magazines were now right before my eyes. I hadn't noticed it from the beach, but now as I walked out on the dock I was amazed at the boats I was seeing. I stepped slowly, taking in all before me. Then I saw Steph coming in, a photograph brought to life. She saw me from a distance and waved. When they arrived at the dock I reached out to help her from the dingy, and she came up on the dock and embraced me enthusiastically. "It's so good to see you. How have you been? You know April left just this morning?"

"I ran into her at the airport," I said, leaving it at that.

"It's too bad she couldn't be here," she said as Joe got out of the dingy. He was a well-tanned and handsome man, forty four to Steph's twenty-six. We were introduced and shook hands. He was polite but didn't look happy, and I didn't seem to make him any happier. They were on their way to the store, and we all went together.

It was still early but people were up and about. Living on a sailboat is like camping out, and everyone had that scruffy campground look except in a tan and well-moneyed way. The prices at the store were in Eastern Caribbean Currency, but even if they were in American dollars they still would've meant nothing to me.

"What do you feel like for breakfast?"

"I don't care," I answered honestly. A more honest answer would've been, "Food."

As I was salivating in the cereal section, she asked, "Is cereal O.K.?" Like a dog being offered a bone, I nodded and tried to keep my tongue from hanging out.

Walking back, I asked about their plans to sail to Europe. Joe and Steph glanced at each other uncomfortably. She said, "It looks like we're not going."

I didn't ask why not, but she continued, "April really threw a monkey wrench into our plans by leaving like she did, and we decided not to go. We've had quite a morning, you know. Did she tell you about it?" I said no. "Well, it wasn't a pretty picture. I mean we had these plans all set, and then she just decided to leave. It really screwed us up. We decided after she left this morning to go to Venezuela and cruise for the summer. We'll be leaving in a few days." Then she added, "Just the two of us."

We got to the dingy and Joe said to me, "You get in and I'll hand you the groceries." I did, and moments later we were motoring out past the nicest boats in the world to a fine Hinkley ketch not upstaged by anything around her. I was welcomed onto the boat as if my presence was taken for granted, which I was very appreciative of since they were in no way obliged to do so. The aft cabin was offered to me, and I put my pack on the berth.

After I had washed up, I came out to the table to find it set with a breakfast right off of a Cheerios box: a bowl of cereal, orange juice, toast and coffee. It was like a dream. I sat at the only place left, which was right beside Steph.

If a person is deprived of sleep for nine days their body starts to produce an hallucinogenic drug much like LSD. If you haven't slept for just one day things can also start to seem a little strange. Maybe my judgement was impaired, but Steph seemed just a little too happy to see me.

She asked about mutual acquaintances and about things in Port Townsend, and really laughed at what I said though I wasn't trying to be funny.

The twinkle in her eye made me uncomfortable. Was she just trying to make me feel welcome? Just a friendly person? I couldn't tell.

"And you have to tell me about Bill," she said.

"Oh, you know Bill," I said, "He's still Bill."

She broke into hysterics. "April talked a lot about you," she said laughing, "But she didn't say you were so charming." I wasn't trying to be charming either.

She put her hand on my wrist. Joe put his eyes on her hand. I put a spoonful of cereal in my mouth. "You know what we have to do?" she asked, squirming down the seat to tell me. He crossed his legs. I tapped my foot.

"What?"

She licked her lips. He blinked his eyes. I cleared my

throat.

"We can pack some lunches and take the tender out to this little beach outside the bay and go swimming and have a little picnic." He sipped his juice. I blinked my eyes. She licked her lips.

He raised one eyebrow. She raised both eyebrows. I lowered both of mine and said,"I was thinking I'd like to take a little nap."

She didn't seem disappointed. "Oh, O.K. I didn't know you were tired." That settled it.

I looked at Joe, but saw neither approval nor disapproval. He held his cereal bowl in his hand like a poker hand, and looked at me from above it without giving any clues as to his thoughts.

I was on his boat eating his food, and now his girlfriend was sitting beside me being flirty. He had already been having a bad day, and I wasn't making it any better. I thanked them for breakfast and went aft to lay down on my berth to sleep on a full stomach.

In a bed again I soon thought of being in bed with Autumn. How easy it would've been to be waking up with her right now, how simple and pleasant. We would spend the morning making love, then have a nice breakfast together, eating my own food in my own place...

Instead we were both miserable, sad, lonely and dejected. I was even feeling a little queazy. It had been a long time since I had slept on a boat. It rocked gently, but incessantly. I was heartsick and sick with uncertainty and sick with regret, and the rocking seemed to concentrate all that sickness at a spot in my chest just below my heart. I could feel it, point to it, press against it, but it did no good. I wanted rest. I wanted to escape into the death of sleep so as to not think, not feel, not remember, and not let that sickness sink down into my stomach and make me puke. I reached into my pack for the seasick pills. I wanted them as a panacea, as heartsick pills and sleeping pills as well. Accidentally, I pulled out the box of rubbers, Trojans. On the box was a black and white picture of a couple walking hand in hand down the beach. The picture taunted me. Their's was a perfect world, I thought. Forever frozen in the moment of walking down the beach on your way to having safe sex. A moment of happiness untouchable by time, unchangeable by bad decisions, complete and never ending. One dozen lubricated latex condom's worth of happiness all rolled up and packaged neatly. I looked at them with loathing and envy in my heart before stuffing them in the bottom of my pack so they could have some privacy. For me it was a Dramamine, and I swallowed it dry.

It wasn't long before the choppy sea of my psyche turned calm, my head set deeper into the pillow, and I began to slip beneath the smooth surface of sleep. I dreamt for a moment that I was walking down the beach. There were two sets of footprints behind me. I reached out beside me for a hand to hold but, there was none. I was all alone. The second set of footsteps had ended some distance back, but there was no one in sight. I looked around and noticed I was naked. Naked except for my penis, which wore a shiny lubricated condom right out of the package. While I looked at it, the condom fell off my penis into the dry sand with a pitiful silence. There was a saltiness in the air that licked at me like a cat's tongue. Even in my dream I could taste it in my mouth and nose as it bathed me like loneliness, and I drifted off into the depths of forgetful sleep.

FIFTEEN

May 2, 1992
6:00 PM

I could've been asleep for two days or twenty minutes. I had no memory of it. I awoke slowly, not sure where, or even who I was. The first solid thing in my head was remorse. "What have I done?" I repeated out loud as a flood of recent memories washed into my mind. Leaning up, I saw from the porthole as beautiful an island scene as is imaginable, but it was all lost on me as I was too busy remembering my despair. I heard someone come down the companionway steps into the galley, then Steph appeared in my cabin. She wore a bikini and a towel wrapped around her waist. Her hair was wet and dripping onto her shoulders and tan back. She didn't notice that I was awake as she got some clothes from under the opposite quarter berth.

"Hi," I said, as she put on a thick robe.

"Hi," she said, as she tied it shut, "Did you sleep well?"

"Great," I said. "What time is it?"

"Dinner time," she spoke with a grin. "Do you like lamb chops?"

"Do I?" I said with enthusiasm. As she left the cabin Joe came down the companionway stairs.

"What were you doing in there?" he asked with hintings of suspicion in his voice.

"Just getting my robe and this dress. I thought I'd wear it tonight."

There was a silence in which I expected to hear, "Likely excuse," but nothing more was said.

I took a three minute (get wet, turn the water off and lather, rinse off) shower and shaved. When I arrived topsides dinner was served, and I felt genuinely good for the first time in two days. I felt it was a fleeting and foundationless good feeling, but that was all I could expect at the time. Joe asked, "Would you like beer or wine with that?" He was drinking a Guiness Stout so I had one too.

Any feelings of unwelcome I sensed may very well have been my own paranoia due to the fact that had he said, "You can't eat my food," or "You can't stay on my boat," then I wouldn't have anything to eat or anywhere to stay. I was in a precarious situation and may have been over-sensitive. I was made to feel welcome, and if sideways glances from his direction kept me concerned, his outward hospitality kept me well fed. And anyway, it was already made perfectly clear that they, like virtually every other boat in the vicinity, would be gone in a matter of days. Any concerns on their part of my infringement on their hospitality would then be solved.

After dinner we went ashore for the last night of festivities. There are actually two parts to English Harbour, and where I had been dropped off was the first part as you approach from the land called Falmouth Harbour. Joe's boat was anchored in Falmouth Harbour. Together we walked to the other part past local souvenir merchants and food stands to get to English Harbour proper, a place called Nelson's Dockyard, where a two thousand person party was already in progress.

Steph and Joe knew that my plans were to now find another boat across the Atlantic, and they had put the word out to their friends during the day. I was introduced to a few captains and boat owners who would be making the crossing, but this evening was for fun and not business, and I was given appointments to meet them the next day.

Yachtsmen are known to uphold many time-tested traditions, and heavy drinking is one of them. Drinking with yachties is like drinking with college freshman on a Friday night. Don't do it unless you're prepared to drink a lot. A round was bought. I ordered a grapefruit soda called Ting and wandered off on my own.

There was an interesting crowd of people there, overlapping and intermingling, but distinct and coming from very different places. There were the big boat owners. These are people who have enough money, usually from undisclosed sources, to buy a magnificent sailboat costing from hundreds of thousands to millions of dollars, who are able to spend all their time sailing their boat or in comparable leisure, and in addition to that, pay a year-round crew livable wages. With them were the glamorous women, distinguishable immediately even in simple clothes by their lofty carriage and "I know you're looking at me" attitude. Women who use their tits like credit cards getting them accepted at the finest resorts all over the world. There were the locals. The ones I saw at English Harbour were the ones whose daily lives were totally given over to serving and providing for us outsiders. If they harbored any animosity of the kind that was vented on me at immigrations, they kept it well hidden. To us they showed the non-person, "I'll be what you want me to be" identity. But they were the invisible ears eyes and heart of the place that would be left when everyone else was gone.

The last and largest group was the sailors. These included the smaller boat owners, crew members (including deckhands and cooks all the way to captains) from the big boats, the charterers down for just a week or two, and periphery characters like me looking for rides.

Joe was a smaller boat owner, though at forty-eight feet his boat would be considered large in most marinas, and Steph was his entire crew.

We all moved out of the way as a little parade of the local marching band made its way through the center of Nelson's Dockyard. They were out of tune and looked to me like a big marching reggae band, but they sounded fun and bright and heralded in the dusk with cheer. Due to their uniforms, I saw them as potential threats to my precious freedom like the immigrations personnel or police, as if one of the trumpet players might at any moment drop his horn and come after me, and I stayed safely out of their view. As they left, the night arrived and with it one less evening between me and whatever was to become of me. The talk around the area was of leaving the next day or the day after and where everyone was going. One thing was clear, everyone was leaving. This place full of boats was about to clear out like a ghost town, to empty likc a draining bathtub.

The idea of going to Spain sat in my mind, but I didn't know how it sat. I actually thought it might be better to turn back and go home, to take that flight to Puerto Rico and take that job at Dunkin' Donuts. Start over from scratch and chalk up this whole trip as experience. The uncertainty I had about taking this trip in the first place followed me all the way to where I wasn't sure I should go. My mind was not at rest. Normally, I might have been social and outgoing and would have met plenty of folks on my own. But I was feeling subdued and uncertain and just wandered aimlessly, open-eyed, and not a little worried.

Darkness brought with it a strange cool southerly breeze. Nighttime was when the real reggae bands came out, as did the nocturnal birds of prey and unless you wanted to see the other side of island life, it was a good idea to be in before too late.

Joe knew which anchor light was his. We powered out on the black water directly to his ketch. Living on a boat, whether it's a raft on the Mississippi or a Schooner in the Bahamas, is the quintessential transient life. The hiker's bed is the solid ground, but the sailor's is flowing water. You live afloat. Where else could you live that your bed rises five feet and turns one hundred and eighty degrees while you sleep? The view from your back door changes for you, but if you still don't like it you just weigh anchor and you're off, all the way around the world if you wish.

The boat was turned around when we got to it. Whereas before looking aft you saw the entrance to the harbor, now you looked across the bay at what I learned was called Cat-Boat Harbour. I asked why it was called this, and Joe said it was because before it was dredged it was a shallow anchorage and only catamarans could stay there.

A catamaran is a boat with two long thin parallel hulls. If the traditional monohull sailboat can be seen as a big phallic symbol with its penile bowsprit thrusting through swells, then you might see the catamaran as the opposite, as the symbolically female boat, caressing spread-legged over the top of the water. Indeed, the monohull is the boat of patriarchal society, of England and Europe, and the catamaran the invention of the more matriarchal South Seas societies. Monohulls are known to be more stable and catamarans much faster. They each have their own benefits, but I think there is something to be learned from the fact that the trimaran, or combination of the male and female qualities, is considered by those without strong prejudices to be the best all-around boat, and they hardly ever sink.

We spent the evening lounging lazily in the cockpit and then in the galley when it got too cool, talking leisurely when the words surfaced, or reading and enjoying the breeze when they didn't.

I retired to my cabin early and thought without resolution about what I should do and without understanding about what I had done, until sleep came to wipe my thoughts away like steam from a window.

SIXTEEN

May 3, 1992
6:30 AM

Boats and horses in the morning are parallel. A field of horses will all turn their sides to the sun, and a bay full of boats will all turn their bow to the wind. They begin their days geometrically aligned with the natural forces of our world.

I had been out of alignment.

I awoke early and went out to the aft deck with my blanket. There was a new clearness in the air and in my head. I had my bearings and understood where I was. It was silly for me to maintain my plans for going to Spain. What would I do with two dollars and a ticket to Puerto Rico from Antigua, in a country where I barely spoke the language? Not only was it stupid from a financial viewpoint, but also from a personal one in that it was contrary to my feelings, my intuition, that little voice inside us all which it is the epitome of stupidity not to listen to.

I knew what I must do, and thus it was easy to map out a course. Antigua is a wintering ground for boats from the east coast of the U.S. as well. I would search for a boat headed for

Maine, or Boston, or my home state Connecticut. From there I would figure out a way back to Port Townsend. With that thought, with that plan of action, my previous alternative of flying back and calling home was dropped and hoped against.

The sun hits the highest masts first, and then makes its way down to the deck and pries into the windows at an ever increasing angle. My hosts were pried out just before eight and came topsides with steaming coffees.

"You're up early," Steph said quietly, as if to not wake the day too fast.

"I've decided to wait on Spain." I said. "Today I'm going to look for boats going north, to New England." It was a clear decision, and they supported it. We ate a peaceful breakfast of fruit, yogurt, and toast. I had a big and important day ahead of me, but it was too early to start yet, so I just let the time lap gently against my bow as it does against a boat at anchor.

Once we motored in it became a race against time. I let out all reefs and ran everywhere I went. There were noticeably fewer boats, and on bulletin boards all around the harbor there were tattered notes from boats needing crew, "For Venezuela, For Greece, For France," and an equal amount from crew needing boats, "Seventeen years blue water experience," or, "Ready to go anywhere in the world." I got the names of some boats going north, one to Florida, one to the Bahamas that said they would fly you back to the U.S. from there, one to Nova Scotia.

The radio traffic was tremendous. They monitor channel 68 and there was hardly a moment's free air space. I shoved my way onto the airwaves, "Xanadu, Xanadu, Xanadu; Limey's."

Limey's was a bar.

I ran the thin strip of land between English and Falmoutn harbours probably a dozen times like some ridiculous example of the work ethic in action against the background of relaxing vacationers and relaxed natives. From Limey's bar to the Yacht Club, from one bulletin board to the next, from one marine radio to another, calling boats, checking leads, putting my name on lists, setting up interviews with captains, asking anyone and everyone if they knew of any boats going to, not Spain, not France, not the warm Mediterranean, but back to North America. Within the first half hour ashore I arranged two interviews, but still I ran from bulletin board to bulletin board looking for something, anything. There were other people like me. People who, however they got there, knew they had to find a way out and fast, and they were doing the same thing.

My first interview was with the captain of the boat going to the Bahamas. His deciding question was, "How much big-boat experience do you have?" Santana 22's didn't fit in that category. I told him about schooner sailing in Maine, though that didn't do much for him either. He said he was looking for someone with a little more "big boat experience," but that he would keep me in mind. Then he went on to tell me at length about the owner's many idiosyncrasies, which I was forced to listen to politely, thinking that maybe what he really wanted was someone with big-mouth experience.

The second was with a couple going to Nova Scotia. They wanted someone who could cook, and said they would really prefer a female.

I ran into another lead and sat in Limey's calling a boat I

heard was going to New York, but got no reply. I called their name, "Tax Shelter, Tax Shelter, Tax Shelter; Limey's," and waited for their call. I called again, sipping cold water but got no reply.

There was a constant drone on the radio. A man with an English accent was repeating over and over again, "Crew member available, crew member available, call Phillip on the Blue Moon.

"...Can go anywhere in the world, call Phillip on the Blue Moon..." It was repeated with a frightening hopelessness.

SEVENTEEN

May 3, 1992
12:30 PM

"Hey mate, I saw that Tax Shelter leavin' early this mornin,'" an Australian man at the bar with a morning Bloody Mary told me. Time was running out. Boats were leaving all the time. Half the notices on the bulletin boards were from boats already gone. Calls to them were just empty echos. I felt my welcome on Joe's boat may have been wearing thin. I had to persist even till all the boats were gone.

I changed my approach. The sea wall there at Nelson's Dockyard is called Slipway. The water is deep there, and boats are lined up stern end in along its whole 400 yard length with barely a space between them. I started at the beginning, knocking on every hull.

"Headed towards Boston or Maine?"

"Brazil."

"Boston or Maine?"

"The Med."

"Boston or Maine?"

"Venezuela."

"Boston or Maine?"

"Portsmouth, New Hampshire, but we've a full crew."

I ran from boat to boat with increasing urgency. Faster I ran, knocked and talked. "Going north?"

"No, sorry."

"North?"

"South."

"North?"

"East."

"Massachusetts?"

"Casablanca."

"Need crew to the U.S?"

"Sorry, we can't help you."

"Headed towards Connecticut?"

"No, but I heard the St. Christopher is going to Rhode Island."

"St Christopher, where's that?"

"You're standing right next to it," he pointed right beside me.

I turned and saw her, the St. Christopher. Forget love at first sight, this was awe at first sight. There's a center area of Slipway where all the grandest boats are, and this was the first boat in that area. All the other boats so far I had knocked on the hull and talked down into the cockpit. It would've been foolish to knock on this hull. It was low tide, and I couldn't even see on deck. Looking up at ten feet of dark blue freeboard, I imagined such a boat at sea. There was the red white and blue flag of the United Kingdom flying from her stern and below it was written in big scrolly red letters, "St Christopher," with the home port given as Inverness, Scotland. St. Christopher, the patron saint of travelers. There was a gangplank onto the deck with a thin chain across it. Not wanting to board without permission, I ran back to Limey's bar, skipping the rest of Slipway.

"Crew position needed, call Phillip on the Blue Moon," was still droning on.

I grabbed the radio and elbowed onto the airwaves, "St. Chistopher, St. Christopher, St. Christopher," I called as if praying. "St. Christopher, St. Christopher, St. Christopher; Limey's," I repeated, and waited for a response.

The radio waxed on with other calls and with, "Phillip on the Blue Moon," then the words, "St. Christopher, Limey's. Turn to channel 72," came through.

"Yes," I said on 72, "I'm calling to see if you need any crew going north."

"We may very well," answered the Australian-sounding woman on the other end. "Why don't you come aboard and talk with the captain, over."

I caught my breath incredulous and looked at myself in the mirror. I wondered how diaphanous my desperation was. Would he see through me? See me not as an able and eager crew member, but as an opportunistic young slouch trying to save his skin? I looked presentable, but would I seem pitiful? I could scarcely tell as I held my shoulders back and tried to recall what it was to feel confidence as I walked up the long gangplank The woman I had just talked to met me on deck. She asked me to take off my shoes and escorted me to the crew mess far forward. Down below was air-conditioned, and it felt good after running around all morning. There wasn't any annoying background noise as is often the case on air-conditioned boats. The generator ran but was silenced in the distant engine room. The crew were busy taking care of last minute provisioning and good-byes. The captain was busy entertaining some farewell guests. I was told to wait for him in the aft bar.

To get to the aft bar I went through the crew mess, past a full size washer and dryer, past the door to the galley, up stairs through the guest lounge, past the guest dining room, (below which was the library with as many books as some small colleges and guest quarters, one of which had a jaccuzi), past the steps up to the large pilot house, to the door of the aft bar, at the aft end of the deck house. The aft bar had large French doors which opened to the expansive aft deck. They were closed at the moment. There was a finely woodworked bar, plush leather chairs, and paintings of famous boats. I felt that it would be most proper for me, as a prospective crew member, to sit in the hardest, most uncomfortable chair, but there weren't any that compromised comfort in any way, so I stood.

The captain wasn't long in coming. He seemed to size me up the moment he saw me and asked me to have a seat. He was a large man with brown hair. In his English accent I discerned the singular confidence of the capable as I was asked various things, including what kind of sailing experience I had. I told him about being a volunteer instructor aboard Santana 22's. He seemed to consider this, then said thoughtfully, "The bow-sprit on this boat is 21 feet long."

He asked what my plans were and I said, "To take a delivery back to the U.S."

"And then what?" he asked.

"Then go back to Seattle."

I seemed to have passed. He said his first mate was gone for the next two weeks and that they needed an extra deckhand for a delivery up to Newport, Rhode Island, but all he could offer was room and board and passage to Rhode Island.

Newport, Rhode Island! The words nearly jumped out of my mouth as I accepted the offer. We shook hands to make it official.

"We're leaving in an hour. Have your things aboard, and be ready to go in forty-five minutes."

Forty five minutes! I was off and running again. At Falmouth I hitched a dingy ride out to Joe's boat. There seemed to be an "oh, you're still here" feel when they saw my feet, but when they saw my face they knew I had good news.

"I got on a boat," I said.

"Which one?" Steph asked, excited.

"Guess."

As I said before, Antigua during race week is the home to some of the greatest sailboats in the world. To sail on any one of them would've been a privilege, but there were those few, the best of the best, and the St. Christopher was one of them. Maybe not *the* biggest or *the* most luxurious, but close to it and favorably comparable with any sailing yacht in the world.

She read the look on my face and guessed the most outrageous and incredible guess, "Not the St.Chistopher!?"

I nodded yes, and she jumped on me with a congratulatory hug, shouting, "I don't believe it!" Joe too beamed happiness as I hustled to my cabin to repack my bag.

They rode me in with their tender, and escorted me aboard the St. Christopher. Joe, whose boat would be considered extravagant in some circles, now seemed to be considering an upgrade.

They were shown around by the cook who was the first to welcome me aboard. Joe asked questions in quick succession like a boy looking at a new toy, and was answered as quickly.

"What's the length and beam?"

"135 feet on deck, 156 over all. Twenty seven feet a-beam."

"Steel construction?"

"Yes, built in Bath, Maine in 1978."

"What are the masts made of?"

"Aluminum. The main mast is 143 feet high and the mizzen 126."

"That's amazing. What kind of engines?"

"We have two Volvo Penta's as engines and two more as generators."

"I don't believe it. Can I see the engine room?"

He was shown the engine room and the pilot house where he was in rapture. "Wow, is that the new GPS?" He wouldn't even touch the global positioning system and just stared at it as one would a prized jewel.

I was nervous and was still trying to make a good impression and was hoping that their presence wouldn't get me kicked off.

"What's the range?" he asked.

"Under sail it's indefinite. Under power at twelve knots we can go 7,400 nautical miles, at eight knots 10,800."

"Un-be-lievable," he said slowly. "Who owns it?"

Almost like a reflex she answered, "We can't say." And that was the end of the questions.

The boat also had a Furuno Radar, full size t.v. and video collection, a restaurant-size refrigerator, two sat-navs, two satellite telephones (the crew line and the private line, each with its own gyro-stabilized satellite dish atop the mizzen mast), an IBM computer, a Xerox copy machine, and a big old single-side band radio that looked like a prop from an old science fiction movie. Later, when I was being shown around in greater detail, I asked, as I held out my new watch conspicuously if they had a sextant on board. "Maybe somewhere," said the deckhand who was showing me around, "I've been on board three years and've never seen one."

Joe turned to me and shook my hand as if he was quite happy the ways things had all turned out. He got a tour of this great boat, and I was out of his hair. I imagined him saying, greatly relieved, as he and Steph left, "That Chris was a really good guy."

"Good to meet you," he said, "and good luck. I'm sure you'll have a great time."

"Thanks for the hospitality," I said, meaning it.

"It was nothing."

"Well that worked out good," Steph said. "Fly down, sleep all one day, get on the St. Christopher the next." She was smiling humorously and hugged me again while Joe looked at the video collection.

They deboarded, and I was given a red crew shirt with a picture of the boat embroidered on the breast pocket above the red scrolly words "St. Christopher" and shown to my cabin.

The deckhand's were berthed two to a room in cabins before the mast. The captain and the stewardess, who had been on the boat the longest, each had their own cabins aft. The seven guest cabins were unused. I was given the top bunk in a cabin with a red-haired South African named Devon. Our's was a starboard cabin and was pretty much the same as the rest of the forward cabins. It had comfortable bunk beds with lee-boards beneath the mattress so we didn't fall out when on a starboard tack. There was one big closet split down the middle and a head for just the two of us featuring a flush toilet, sink and shower. "How long are the showers limited to?" I asked.

"Shower as long as you want, mate. We have a water-maker on board that makes three thousand gallons a day."

I stowed my small pack in the closet, hung the shirt I was wearing on the hook, and put away my shoes, not to touch them again for two weeks. I went above as the gang plank was being brought back on board and the two-inch thick dock lines being taken in and stowed in the aft lazerette.

EIGHTEEN

May 3, 1992
2:00 PM

My circumstances were suddenly very different. I was on deck wearing a crisp red crew shirt. I was no longer on the periphery looking in but was inside being looked at by everyone who had come to see this grand ship leave. People waved to us as we motored out of the harbor, and I waved back as if it were my own.

We set sail immediately. The St. Christopher was a staysail ketch. She had six sails totaling 9,250 square feet. From the stern they were the mizzen sail, mizzen staysail, main fisherman (the sail in the space above the mizzen staysail coming aft from the main mast), main staysail, jib, and jib topsail, called the jib-top for short. She was tended to by twelve full-time crew. These were the captain, the first mate presently on leave, the boatswain, the ship's carpenter, the cook whom I met at first, the stewardess who served the meals and took care of other domestic duties, the ship's engineer who ironically was from Scotland like Star Trek's Scotty, and five deckhands.

While I was on board for the delivery we were without a first mate, and the boatswain and ship's carpenter served as deckhands. I was the only American. The engineer was Scottish, the captain, cook, and one deckhand were English. The stewardess and boatswain and two deckhands were Australian, another deckhand was South African, the ship's carpenter and the last deckhand were from New Zealand. It was like Winston Churchill's three volume *History of the English Speaking Peoples* (excepting Canada), live and in the flesh.

Once all sail was set we headed 315 degrees on the gyro-stabalized compass, fifty five degrees off the wind, at ten and a half knots in a twenty-knot breeze for the island of St. Maartin. I looked to one of my mates, "What do we do now?" I asked.

"Gweet at five, till then whatever you want."

I later learned that there were two terms used in reference to food. "Jeet?" translated as, "Did you eat?" and "Gweet," which was the answer to the negative when asked "Jeet?" and meant "Go eat."

Do what I want? Three hours ago I didn't know where I'd find myself the next day and now I had two and a half hours of free time aboard a world class yacht before dinner! I sauntered softly forward, not wanting to break the spell or wake from the dream, and climbed out on the bowsprit. The bowsprit that had been forbidden me on the Mary Day. It was a much longer bowsprit than that boat and over the warm Caribbean, not cold, dark Penobscot Bay. I sat on it in disbelief, barely understanding my situation, like a monkey on a space ship.

Five o-clock rushed on, and I went below in the same daze that had held me above. As I stepped down the steep companionway into the crew mess, the stewardess said to me, "Good'ay Chris, would you like tea or coffee?"

It was all too amazing. I said, "Coffee," my words soft so as not to burst the bubble of this dream. I felt I was pushing it when I asked, "With extra cream, please?" The feeling of potential incarceration was still a sensitive insecurity in my heart. I thought they may as soon say, "Hey, I saw you lose all your money in Puerto Rico," as give me cream. I sat down at the table, and she put the coffee and cream before me politely.

Soon one platter of Beef Wellington and one of au grautin potatoes were placed at the center of the table, on one side of them a pitcher of Tang (no kidding), and on the other a basket of bread. After that night of fasting at the police station, food had taken on a different quality for me. I ate sparingly and slow, while my mates shoveled it in.

"You don't eat like an American," one of them said, a noodle hanging from his mouth.

"How do Americans eat?" I asked.

"Like bloody slobs."

After dinner the captain arranged the watch schedules and put the deckhands into one group of three and another of four. I was in the four with the two New Zealanders and an Australian. There were to be three four-hour watches and two six hour watches in a twenty-four hour period broken up, starting at 8:00 AM as follows: 8 to 2, 2 to 8PM, 8 to midnight, midnight to 4, and 4 to 8AM. Breakfast, lunch and dinner were served when the daytime watches overlapped, respectively at 8:00 AM, 2:00 PM and 8:00 PM. One watch would eat before they came on and the other when they got off.

We were sailing to St. Maartin where we would stop for a day before heading for Newport, R.I. My watch group was to go on at eight so, unbelievably, I had even more free time aboard this great boat after dinner.

I went back out to the bowsprit and laid down in the netting facing wide-eyed forward.

...I remember the first day I saw it, that far off place. It was years ago. I was sailing in Monterey Bay, California, where I had sailed dozens of times before, this time in an Olson 30. There were two of us.

There was a steady easterly and, after getting close hauled until the gunwales were in the water and doing a few figure eights, we found ourselves on a course heading due west. We each drifted off into our own space, as is possible out on the water even in a boat that small. My friend was reclined in the cockpit with his sunglasses on, steering with his big toe, smiling slightly and basking in the hypnotic beauty of the day as if on a strong opiate. I was sitting beneath the spinnaker pole, cross-legged on the foredeck like a Buddist in meditation, facing west.

With home fading in the distance behind and nothing but the horizon ahead, I swear I could almost see paradise. It was just beyond the horizon, that perfect place of our dreams where everything is as it should be. A place of beauty and justice. The place we had know of as children but since seem to have forgotten. I saw shimmering crystal cities and glowing women with bright eyes, flowing clear water and sunshine, everything wonderful and good. It was the world of my dreams just beyond the horizon. I imagined how it could bring one ever again to the sea, around and around the world in search of that perfect place. I wanted to go to it, westward to the horizon never looking back, follow the sun to the place of love and beauty.

We had two sandwiches, a bottle of water, and twelve beers; how I wanted to go! We had a compass, but no radio or even electricity; I couldn't turn back! I could almost see the tops of its mountains, hear the sweet strains of its music. Forward, forward, I had to press on. Look back and turn to a pillar of salt, lifeless and dry. We would find paradise or die trying. I was at sea and the world was mine to create. How could I even think of turning back?

By the time we looked, California was a thin shadow behind us. He eased the boat around. I wanted to stick my finger into the compass and stop the needle on "W," west, 270 degrees. I wanted to keep it pointing towards the sun and us along with it. The spell was broken as we headed back, but the memory remained indelible and clear.

The wind began to freshen the moment we headed home as if it didn't approve of our decision. It pounded us with the words, "Go see, go see," as the two of us struggled against it in that Ultra Light Displacement Boat. We arrived back at the marina well after dark, cold, soaking wet, thoroughly worn out and somehow sad.

It was there again as I laid parallel to the bowsprit, safe in the netting of St. Christopher, facing forward like a living maidenhead, high and dry over the crashing bow, and not heading back as the sky grew darker but heading forward, forever forward.

At eight o-clock I went on watch. Heading for St. Maartin,

we were still doing ten knots in a twenty-knot breeze, still on a close reach about 55 degrees off the wind on a compass heading of 315 degrees. There was nothing in sight, not a light on the horizon, not a star in the sky, not a blip on the radar within a twenty five miles. Just us and the sea.

On my first watch my mates and I were new acquaintances, but I looked forward with keen interest to the deep talks we would have during the long watches to come.

One thing some people don't consider when planning long ocean voyages is how boring it can be. They get out to sea and look at the horizon, featureless in all directions, and at the chart, equally featureless for most of the way around the globe, and say, "I've saved fifty years for this?" A month after they broke a bottle against the hull they're putting an ad in *Sail* magazine saying, "Make offers on this World cruiser, no expenses spared, barely used," or else, "Divorce forces sale."

I was afflicted with no such boredom. I went out and checked the sheets, walked the aft deck like a sea captain of old, and hung my head off the side to see the wondrous phosphorescence in the water and hear the fizzing of sea foam from our bow wave tickling in my ear. Around midnight the sky cleared for a moment, and I caught a glimpse of the North Star, low on the horizon, just off our starboard bow. We were at about seventeen degrees north latitude. Newport is about forty-two. Come near dear Polaris, I thought, I am heading to you, my friend.

NINETEEN

May 4, 1992
5:10 AM

At 4:00 AM I was on my first dawn watch, and St. Maartin lights were in sight. While the world slept we were looking alive and handing (taking down) sail. The wind was fresh and the air felt clean. The whole experience was exhilarating. As dawn snuck up on the horizon, we lowered our anchor and were let off watch. Breakfast was moved to nine. My first full day as a crew member and we were being given a day's leave to go shopping ashore.

After a little sleep, I came out of my cabin just before nine to the question, "Coffee again today, Chris?"

"Tea, please," I asked. Having just come from the Seattle area I was used to quite good coffee, and the freeze dried stuff with non-dairy creamer I was given the day before was appreciated but not very good. The breakfast served was toast, sausage, bacon, eggs, and the ever present Tang. Over the meal the captain asked, "Is there anyone who doesn't want to shop today?" My wallet certainly wasn't making a dent in the shelf.

I said I probably wouldn't be doing much shopping. "Good, then you can ride us in on the tender." This brought a subdued derision from the rest of the crew, as if I was tricked into an undesirable job. Little did they know.

The tender was an eighteen-foot solid bottomed Zodiac with inflatable sides and a 150 horsepower engine. We lowered it on the davits into the clear blue water, and the captain and five others got in and sat on the thick inflated sides. In the middle was a long thin seat like a motorcycle, except with a steering wheel instead of handlebars. For some reason they thought I knew how to drive one of those things. I straddled the seat like an old pro and found the throttle control by my right knee. In the interview he asked me about sailing experience, not powerboating experience. I had once taken the wheel of a Boston Whaler for a second on a lake in Connecticut while my friend lit a cigarette. Other than that, powerboats and I were strangers.

Someone primed the engine and said, "O.K." It had a key and on the throttle it said "Faster, Slower, Start," and "Reverse." I already knew how to use a steering wheel. How hard could the rest be? I put it in "Start" and turned the key. It started right away, and I felt as proud as if I had invented the engine myself. I eased it into motion, and we were off smoothly and without worry.

"Don't be shy there, Chris," the captain said. "At this rate, by the time we get there we'll have to come back."

He asked for it, I thought, and I popped it into "Faster" like Mario Andretti coming into a straightaway. The engine responded like a demon, and we immediately shot off, the bow shot up high as the engine dug into the water, and the captain in his Sunday best very nearly fell off. He grabbed onto the arm of the cook, and they nearly fell off together. Luckily they regained their balance, and I wasn't thrown off at St. Maarten.

I went back for the rest of the crew and made arrangements to meet them in four hours. I backed the boat away from the little dock there at Philipsberg, St Maarten, and pointed it towards the St. Christopher. The scene in front of me was of dozens of fine sailboats at anchor in a clear blue tropical bay, with the St. Christopher dwarfing them all at anchor half a mile out. "Deride me for this?" I thought, as I opened up the throttle and zipped, not to that quaint schooner, not to that cute sloop, but to the St. Christopher, towering above them all. Once away from the other boats I pushed it as fast as it would go and blazed out far beyond the St. Christopher, jumping over the choppy water like a skipped stone, all the way to where I could feel the ocean swells. I slowed the boat down and turned it around like a jet pilot who had just shot up to 60,000 feet. I was high in the sky, and those boats at anchor were little things like cars as seen from the top of a tall building. I gunned the motor again and headed back even faster. I was ducked down like a motorcycle racer and bouncing off the water like a speedboat, as light blues and aquamarines rushed before my eyes. The boats, the beach, the island were all rushing towards me in the unreal colors of animation as I dove in with the heat of re-entry scalding my eyes and the spray flying from my stern like flames from a rocket. It was like a great big video game, except this video game I could smell, taste, and feel splashing against my skin. This a video game involved all the senses. I was living and breathing it. This was the real thing.

Eventually, I tied the tender to the St. Christopher like a tired horse and climbed aboard, all alone, like it was, dare I say it: my boat. I walked the aft deck, the fore deck, I climbed the outer shroud like Irving Johnson rounding Cape Horn aboard the Peking and stood on the first spreader, climbed on to the second, on to the third (of four) and stopped there, seventy-five feet above the decks. I surveyed the scene like a king might his kingdom, and breathed the air deeply. I descended via the stepped mast and went out to the bowsprit. The water was clear and warm, very inviting. I stripped to my shorts and dove in like Adam in Paradise, swimming around to the tender and climbing back aboard to repeat the baptism many times. I swam around in front of the boat as if in a backyard pool, and napped in the cradle of the bowsprit netting like a baby. I tried to read my book, but it required too much work. This, after all, was a day off.

Four hours flew by, and soon I was again pulling up to that same dock. As I tied off the boat a tourist from New Jersey said to me, "Did you just come from that big blue boat out there?" I nodded yes, squinting up at him in the bright thin clouds. "It's quite a boat," he said.

"It sure is," I agreed.

The crew came back one by one, looking like families at a mall before Christmas. St. Maarten was a shoppers' paradise, a duty-free port, and they took complete advantage of it. Because of all the added baggage, it took three trips to bring them back. Once on the boat, they spread their booty on the galley table like pirates after a raid. It was then I learned that the deckhands made one thousand dollars a month, room and board included. All they had to pay for on the boat were phone calls. When I heard that I felt like asking the captain, "How about just fifty bucks or something?" but I refrained. All the stuff couldn't fit on the table. There were watches, cameras, portable stereos, jewelry, three people bought hand-held video cameras for six hundred dollars that I later saw priced at $1,900 in the States. The cook bought a bottle of the exact same 1987 French bordeaux I had considered buying before I came. In Washington it cost forty-two dollars. There, it was twelve-fifty. The words "duty-free" were on my tongue, and I salivated greedily.

It was all soon packed away to make room for a quick lunch before preparing to leave. At lunch the captain asked, "Were you up the mast while we were gone?" A sudden shock of guilt and vulnerability rushed in my veins. I said, "Yes sir."

"That was right ambitious of you," he said, with an approving gleam in his eye; then said to the rest of the crew with a laugh, "I looked out at the boat and saw him climbing the rigging like a pirate!"

As we prepared to leave, I was given the job of flaking the anchor chain as we hoisted it to go. If derision was undeserved earlier, it was appropriate now. I was the newest crew member, and this was the least desirable job. I was shown to the forward storage or "forward store" and the space where the anchor chain came in. There was 150 feet of rode (chain) out and at least three times as much available. Also in the forward store were two surf boards, many gallons of paint, various caustic cleansers, and a large tool chest. It was an area about twelve feet across and large enough to stand in, and was beneath the two most forward cabins. I was shown how to do it and told to wait. Each link of this chain was as big as both my fists together. I had never seen any so large, and thought it should have a name all to itself. "Chain" just didn't do it justice. Soon it came pouring through a hole in the ceiling like an evil spring, and I flaked it back and forth as I had been shown. It really wasn't that bad of a job at first. It required some exertion, but that was welcome. Then the chain that was on the bottom came up. They tried to hose most of the mud off as it came in, but it still got pretty messy. I was in St. Maartin- bottom mud up to my arms by the time all the rode was in, the anchor was weighed safely in the cats-head, and we were off.

I climbed out of the forward store wiping my hands on my new crew shirt, and the stewardess said, "Be sure to give that to me when you're through." I did, with an apology and the next day it showed up on my bed cleaned and folded.

When I went above after changing my shirt, all sail was set, and we were off to a new world, pointing sixty degrees off the wind on a compass heading of 340 degrees, destination: Newport, Rhode Island. That night I went to bed with my hands tender and throbbing from climbing the rigging, hanging from the bob stays, hauling the tender up with the davits, and sheeting the sail. Irving Johnson said in his book that they went to bed every night with throbbing hands and wrists. I was prepared to accept no less.

TWENTY

May 5, 1992
2:15 PM

By the middle of the third day out of St. Maartin our days fell into a regular routine. The rotation of the watches made it so that we were on watch at all different times of the day. I liked it best when we were on the 4:00 to 8:00 AM shift for the sunrise, because that meant we would also be on during the sunset shift of 2:00 to 8:00 PM. There were two things that had to be done every hour, a few occasional duties, and one thing that had to be done at all times.

Once every hour someone had to do an engine check. This entailed taking a clipboard down to the engine room, putting on headphones to save your ears, opening the pressure-sealed door, and climbing down a ladder into the brightly lit and clean engine room. The four green Volvo Pentas were arranged like the four diamonds on a playing card, with just enough room between them for a man to walk comfortably. The two forward engines were used as generators, the two aft ones turned the five-foot diameter propeller. One of the generators was running at all times, and they were switched about every eight hours. In the engine room you were under the water line. That kept the room from getting too warm and gave it, to me at least, a solid cavernous feeling, especially when wearing those muffling headphones. First thing to do was check the fuel in the tank. I don't know how big the main tank was, but the holding tank held one hundred gallons. If it got below fifty we would have to turn some valves and knobs and fill it up from the main tank. Next we would check the running engine's control panel and the ship's electric control panels to be sure all the levels and temperatures were O.K. and that no warning lights were lit. Then we would look at the running engines from all angles checking for oil leaks, and wave our hands over them slowly like a magician over a levitated woman, to be sure there were no exhaust leaks, and listen to be sure it sounded well. Also, the water tank levels and the water maker had to be monitored. The water maker was a clean, new and very simple looking device; white, blue, shiny and very mysterious to me. I understood reverse osmosis when I read about it in the water maker's manual; but when I looked at that compact device, I couldn't understand how it worked so well, making three thousand gallons of good tasting water from salt water every twenty-four hours. At the aft end of the engine room were the seven bilge pumps which we had to prime and turn on one by one, and if there was any pressure, wait till it ended and all the water was pumped from whichever bilge had some. Next to the bilge pump valves was the shaft break which kept the prop from turning the shaft while we sailed. During the one windless afternoon when we were under power, we also had to check the shaft bearings in shaft alley. Shaft alley was the deep gut of the boat. It was through another pressure-sealed door heading aft out of the engine room. When you went through it and closed the door, everything was again quiet and it was darker and cooler than the engine room. If the St. Christopher was a high school then shaft alley was where kids would sneak to smoke cigarettes and feel secretive and private. The jacuzzi water was kept in a tank there while we were under way. When powering, we had to make sure the shaft bearings didn't overheat. When under sail, you could just go there and breathe the free air of a moment's solitude before going back above. The engine room check was a one-man job and once you had it down it took about ten minutes. Never in the whole time I was aboard was there ever anything awry, never even any water in the bilges.

The other hourly task was the log entry. In a thick well-bound ledger book going back one year with one page for each day, twenty-four rows for the hours, and a dozen or so columns, we recorded the simple information which when seen over a few hours can begin to indicate trends. We recorded boat speed and direction, wind speed and direction, sea conditions, sky conditions, temperature, barometric pressure, and there was a large space for comments which was most often blank, but when it was filled was usually interesting in an understated sort of way -"gusts to 60," or "past the Azores to port," or, as written while in the middle of the Atlantic; "radio contact with 20-foot sloop Defiance." The only note written in that space while I was aboard was, "284 miles in 24 hours!" but we haven't gotten that far yet.

The occasional duties were: checking the standing and

running rigging, the spreaders, the bowsprit, bob-stays, dolphin striker, running-back stays, davits, lifelines, the trim of the sails, maybe sheeting in or out a bit here or there. Basically just wandering around the boat looking for something to do. The other occasional duty was making coffee. During the day we could just call down on the intercom to the stewardess to make us a tray of coffees, but at night we got to do it ourselves.

What had to be done at all times was a maintained awareness of the boat. Keeping an eye out, an ear out, even the soles of your feet out for something that might not be quite right, and may be hinting at bigger problems on their way. You look at the radar, look at the horizon, listen to the wind in the rigging, feel the motion with your feet, even smell the air appraisingly. But here was where it became evident that this boat was just too big. On a smaller boat you can feel if she's heeling funny, or if the helm responds in a strange way. We didn't even steer this boat, but just left it on auto-helm all the time except when we were bored enough to take the helm, which basically just meant holding it because the boat steered herself quite well. Even coming about on this boat was like turning on a train. There was no strong motion or boom barely missing your head, no excitement of the foresail shooting across the deck. It was all very steady and practiced.

There is a cohesion on small boats, a connection one feels with the crew and with the boat itself. This boat was too big for that. Maybe I wasn't aboard long enough but even those who had been seemed vaguely impersonal, like city dwellers. If you meet someone from New York City and say, "I lived in New York for nine years," they say, "So fuckin' what." Whereas if you meet someone in whose little hometown in Minnesota you once stopped for coffee, it's a cosmic connection. That is the difference between big boats and small boats. This boat may not have been a New York City but it was a Seattle, and Seattle is too big for me.

It was big enough to get lost on as one can get lost in a big society and fall through the cracks alone and forgotten, as society powers on with them floundering in the wake behind. This, in fact is what bothered me the most -falling off.

If the boat were going ten nautical miles an hour, which it often was, and I went to look around, which I often did, and fell off the stern, my splash probably wouldn't be heard way up in the pilot house above all the other sailing noises. Also, I wouldn't be missed for at least ten minutes, at which time my watch mates would think, "Chris must be off making coffee." By then the boat would be over a mile away. Ten more minutes I would be three miles off the stern, and they would wonder where their coffee was and come looking for me. At first they wouldn't find me and would look closer, my bunk, the engine room, etc. Then, when they didn't find me, they would call the captain and stop the boat. By this time the boat would be about five miles away, and far out of sight to me at water level. If I'm lucky, the water is warm and they can get the boat back to the precise spot they were and find me. If I'm sort of unlucky, the water is cold and I die the peaceful death of hypothermia. If I'm really unlucky, the water is warm, but they underestimate how long ago I fell off, and come back only far enough for me to see them but not enough to see me. I watch them search. I yell as I bob up on the swells until I can yell no more. After two hours they give me up for dead and sail away out of sight.

I don't mean to treat this subject lightly. The fear of falling off was almost always with me in some way. I didn't consider it a phobia or irrational fear. While I was a volunteer sailing instructor, we were supposed to instill in our students an informed respect for how hard it can be for a boat to turn around and get an overboard person back aboard. (And this was in a twenty-two foot boat going five knots in a bay, not a 156 footer doing ten and a half on the ocean.) Also, for how easy it is for someone to die after falling in. We would throw a ring buoy overboard, and it often took the classes three or four tries before they could stop the boat next to the buoy and bring it on board. Plenty of time for it to drown or get hypothermia. I was worried by how often I imagined myself in that buoy's position, as if I was adding to my chances of falling in by "creatively visualizing" it. I tried to shake the thoughts from my mind.

TWENTY-ONE

May 6, 1992
2:30 PM

Watch started at 8:00 AM this day. We were kept busy continuously sheeting out the six sails because the wind was slowly shifting aft and lightening considerably. A lunch of roast beef sandwiches, vegetable soup, and french fries was served at 2:00 PM. All lunches and dinners aboard were of meat and potatoes. I don't know if it was by preference of the cook, captain or some ancient nautical tradition. It may have had something to do with the owner, whoever he was. One evening, after a lamb chop and baked potato dinner, the cook said to the stewardess, "Chuck would've liked that dinner." I wouldn't have thought anything of the comment, but then they both reacted nervously because I was there, and said, "That's not his real name. That's just our nickname for him." Chuck, obviously, was the owner of the boat. Was it Prince Charles? Was it Charlton Heston? Their worry was unnecessary. Who owned the boat was the least of my concerns. Though I found it unbelievable when they said he only used it for a few weeks out of the year, and wanted it in Newport because he was planning a weekend there the coming summer.

At 2:30 I was on deck again, off watch, enjoying the fine weather. I stood next to the captain and a member of the other watch. With the lighter winds aft, I squinted up into the sky and casually said something to the effect of,

"...good spinnaker weather." To which he replied, "Sure is. Too bad we don't have one." Then, as if remembering, he said, "But we do have the queens fisherman and the genoa. We could put them up if you feel energetic." He looked to me as if to say, "Do you?" and I gave an enthusiastic, "Sure."

He turned to the mate on the other side of him and said, "You guys get up that queens fisherman and the genoa."

On the list of how to gain instant unpopularity with the rest of the crew, being responsible for making them do more work than they have to is quite high.

My mate said, "Yes sir," and went aft to tell his watch what they had to do. Not being on watch, I didn't have to help, and as it turns out there wasn't much I could do without really knowing the process. The queens fisherman is a rectangular sail that goes in the space between the two masts where the mizzen staysail and the main fisherman usually are. Its head is sheeted through the fisherman tackle at the top of the mizzen mast, and the foot through the staysail tackle. The sheets were one-inch line. Having one big sail instead of two sails in that space more efficiently catches the wind. The genoa takes the place of the jib top and the jib, the main staysail staying set. I helped carry the 140-foot queens fisherman out of the lazerette and forward to the main mast, but that was about all I could do. Except watch, and watch I did. The sail was brought out with lengths of nylon string wrapped around it, tied at three foot intervals. To my surprise, it was also hoisted up the mast like that. I felt like saying, "You forgot to take off the ties," but decided that quiet observation was best. The main fisherman was taken down, wrapped with that same string and stowed. The mizzen staysail was wrapped on its boom with sail ties. The heavy sail was hoisted up partly by hand, but then was wrapped around the one-foot diameter electric winch for the majority of the way up the mast. I was at the base of a 143-foot mast looking up into the dizzying rigging that even in those light winds seemed may topple at any moment, tearing down from the sky like tree limbs in a hurricane. The sail reached the lofty top of its groove, and the halyard was cleated. To break the nylon ties, the upper sheet was pulled with the mizzen winch. Nylon string can be pretty strong, I thought, as with much effort the winch broke the first wrapping, exposing a small triangle of sail way up there. With more effort, another two were broken. There was a moment's pause before with an amazing sound and show of power, the wind caught the bit of exposed sail and burst it open in thrilling 3-D, coming at me down the mast and filling with a booming crash of bright white sail, like an instant bomb of sunshine exploding massively before my eyes. This breaking out of the sail, as it was called, took my breath away, and I felt like applauding. And if that wasn't enough, the genoa still had to be set.

The other watch lowered the jib and jib top, and tied them to the bowsprit with sail ties. They hanked on the genoa to the foremost forestay. I offered to help, even tried to, but my efforts were like adding insult to injury, and were unwelcome. The huge genoa was hanked on and raised and was to be broken out. One mate took the working sheet and wrapped it around a winch. I laid beside the bowsprit on the two foresails which had just been taken down. Again, the sail exploded above me with awesome force and thundering noise, and this with only a light wind. Such is the latent strength of the wind!

I was thoroughly satisfied. What a sight! What an experience! I went below to write about it in my journal while the adrenalin was still in my blood. I passed through the galley on my way to my cabin. The cook was talking. "I've been on this boat five years and that queen's fisherman's not been up once." It looked awfully nice, I thought, but then I saw that she was directing her words towards me, and was not happy about it. Not that it affected her, it was the principle of the thing. I soon learned that if earlier I was a freshman on a boat full of juniors and seniors, I was now a freshman that nobody liked. One of my watch mates added with disgust, "and that genoa's not been up in a year and a half." I had unknowingly committed a faux paus, but their disapproval could not smother my excitement; it only coupled it with disappointment. It was a disappointment I was already feeling in my fellow crew members.

The true sailor is a rarity today. People in the Navy aboard aircraft carriers the size of small towns are called sailors. Pleasure-seeking yachties, idlers even when active, are called sailors. But to sail for pleasure is different than sailing for work, just ask Joseph Conrad. And there aren't many chances to earn a living sailing anymore. I thought the crew would be lovers of the sea, and of the beauty and work of sailing; but though they may have liked it, they were primarily people interested in a life of leisure, spent lounging in the sun sipping margaritas. "Life's a beach." They wanted to party and have fun, to relax, recreate, not create. Deliveries were not fun. The only reason there was room for me on the boat was because the first mate picked this time for his two-weeks vacation and was flying to Newport. A delivery was work, and he didn't want to have anything to do with it. I learned that the crew's usual duties were to keep the boat clean and polish the brass. They considered this sailing business a pain in the ass. What was to me a one of a kind opportunity, a truly rare experience, was to them just burdensome toil. They wanted to be in port working on their tans and impressing the local girls with tales of high sea adventure. Electric winches for the sheets and halyards, auto helm, not a stitch of rowing or swabbing, tarring the stays, greasing the mast, no real work at all, except waking up and sitting on deck; and they were moody and unpleasant about it virtually the whole trip. My enthusiasm was seen as inappropriate bordering on stupid. I wanted to inspire them to experience their lives, to live them to the fullest and see the wonder which surrounded, them but I was the lowest man on the crew and in no position to lecture. And now I was an unpopular lowest member. Later, at dinner I was ignored like a tattle-tale at recess by my watch mates, and scoffed at by the others as we went on and they got off of watch. Unfortunately, the wind didn't pick up until after our watch, so the other watch got to take the sails down, too.

With the enthusiasm of the sails breaking out still fresh with me, I went to my cabin to write it down. I got my pack out of my closet and opened it to take out my journal. There, I found that box of condoms, rubbers as they used to be called, staring me in the face again. I picked them up, annoyed at the sight of them. They used to be called rubbers when they were talked about mainly by men. Say "rubbers" to a twenty-two-year-old girl, and she barely knows what you're talking about. People don't even wear them on their feet anymore.

It's funny how this thing that has remained virtually the same has changed so much in our minds and our lives. Once, young men kept them hidden in their wallets like a rare and valuable coin which they couldn't wait to spend. Now, they are given out by school nurses, and litter the bottom of girls' purses like spare change. Once, parents were shocked to see them in their children's possession. Now they worry if they don't. Once they brought to mind images of babies or trips to the doctor for a shot of penicillin in the ass, now they make you think of dying young, anal sex, and every person the person you're sleeping with has ever slept with.

How things have changed. What person fifty years ago could've imagined a day when talk of stormy international relations hinted at instant death in eight minutes from an unknown finger on a small red button; when a beautiful warm day could be construed as a sign of the deadly greenhouse effect; when a common cold makes you think you may be dying of AIDS, and that in two years you'll be skin and bones in a hospital bed, another emaciated statistic, while your family stands around thinking, "I wonder if he was gay?" A time when, amidst such amazing medical advancements, a young man can look in the mirror and wonder if he's going to die, not in a war for some cause, not in an accidental car wreck, but for making love with a woman spontaneously on the beach without "pro-tection." Looking in the mirror at twenty-two and wondering when the slow sickly decent will begin. Who could imagine such a thing?

I thought of Autumn being on the pill, and then I just thought of Autumn. Had I only not left her, I thought, we'd be having a nice cool day together right now, so simple and smooth. Money in the bank, and no disgruntled crew to worry about. I should have settled for that life, I thought. I should've quit while I was ahead, been happy with what I had. But then I thought, what about all this great sailing, and this amazing boat? Look at the experience I'd be missing.

I heard a muffled "Oh, sure," coming from somewhere. I thought again of Autumn, then I heard it again, "Su-u-ure," it said. I looked around, and saw that it came from the unopened box of condoms. Again they were taunting me. "Who do you think you're kidding?" they asked. "You know you came here to get together with April. Why else would you have bought us? You picked us up before that box of pills. We know, we were there..."

"Shut up," I said.

"Hey, don't get defensive. It's not our fault you got rejected. Just keep wishin' for the past back, because you sure screwed up your present."

"Shut up!" I said as I stuffed them back into my pack, while they said, "Don't forget, we have an expiration date!" I threw the pack hard into the closet. They were right, I thought. Despite this great sailing opportunity and all the experiences I was having, I was disappointed things hadn't worked out with

April. Though we only knew each other a short while, I felt a certain connection with her, like we were meant for each other. I was taking a chance in coming to see her, and I lost. I had imagined a life for us together, a sunny home with fruit in a bowl. We would taste of the ripeness of life, traveling about the world with someplace to come home to. Stability and adventure. The vagabond with a permanent address. It didn't seem like too outrageous of an idea, like too much to ask. I guess I was wrong. It wouldn't be the first time.

TWENTY TWO

May 10, 1992
4:00 AM

In a vivid dream, I was standing with Autumn on an arched suspension bridge overlooking a dark stormy sea. Ominous clouds hung low overhead. There was no lightning, only rain and a wind strong enough to almost knock us down. We were arm in arm on this bridge, holding onto each other with one arm and onto the bridge with the other for support against the storm. I looked out on the water and saw a small green sloop, double-reefed and flying a storm jib. The boat was rocking terribly, and pounded against a ruthless opposing sea. "Look at that boat," I said, pointing at it and shouting because of the wind. "I'm glad I'm not on that boat. I'd be seasick if I was on that boat." In fact, even just looking at it was making me queasy in my dream. Then I was awakened by a knock on my door. "On watch in five minutes," and I opened my eyes to find that I really was on that boat. The bow of the St. Christopher pounded against the waves like a huge hammer pounding steel. It was so loud I couldn't believe I slept through it. The boat rose and fell violently, crashing as if the water were stone and may shatter the boat to pieces. That was when the scene with the condoms and the Dramamine and my bunk mate bursting in took place. It's better to take them early, I reckoned, because if you're too late there's no way you're going to keep then down. I wouldn't have had a chance to take them later anyway, because in twenty minutes I was strapped in at the bowsprit, doused underwater repeatedly with the rise and fall of the boat, and in no position to come below and take a pill.

As I said, my bunk mate burst in and got under the covers all wet. I pulled myself up through the narrow door to our cabin to find my watch mates getting into foul weather gear and safety harnesses. A safety harness is a very important piece of equipment which you strap to yourself and hook to the boat in heavy weather, so that if a wave washes over the deck, it doesn't take you along with it. One thing I was bothered by was the fact that the foul weather gear was custom-made and matched the boat. It was dark blue with white trim. If any combination of colors is invisible in a choppy sea, especially at night, this is it. It almost makes one rather get wet. Once dressed, we rushed above to relieve the rest of the previous watch. They evacuated the tumultuous topsides without so much as a "Hello" or "Good luck," leaving the captain alone in the deckhouse. He was the symbol of competence, and didn't rest until the boat was safe. I went above to a scene wholly new to me. The kind of sailing I had previously done was the kind where, if it looks too nasty out then you stay ashore. But this was a journey, not a day sail. There was no shore on which to stay. We were six hundred miles from the nearest land, and there was no turning back, turning in, or going home. There's only one thing to do, and that is cope. This may be a small world, but a person can get into some pretty big situations. The scene was one from sailing stories of old. It was the eternal sea, the one you've read about, heard about, seen on t.v, rearing her hard face and rolling her strong shoulders. She hasn't gone away, we just don't get the opportunity to see her so often anymore. I was amazed and enthralled. The wind howled like thrown knives, cutting at our exposed cheeks. We weren't there five minutes before we were all soaked with heavy spindrift. The decks were slanted and awash, but the captain was undaunted, even casual. The force nine winds which had me entranced were nothing new to him.

"Last watch they reefed the mizzen and handed the fisherman. You guys go get that jib top, she's heeling too much," he said, as if asking us to get him a coffee.

Myself and another ran out to the bowsprit to tie up the sail, while the other two took the halyard and the sheet. We clamoured onto the bowsprit, and hooked in our safety harnesses. This was the bowsprit I had laid on just yesterday as in a hammock, a comfortable fifteen feet above the water as the boat rode the swells in a motion so gently that sleep was less desirable. This same bowsprit was now thrashed up and down, rising to nearly forty-five feet over the water, then crashing down to three feet under, engulfing us in frothy salt water that was far warmer than the razor cold northerly wind we were beating against, and the cutting sea spray that slashed at our faces. The swells were shortly spaced, and hit the boat three at a time giving her a violent uncomfortable motion. St. Christopher was made for majestic ocean journeys on great rising swells she could ride over with elegance and graceful power, not short battering ones like these. We crashed underwater four times, my mate once being washed partly overboard. He would've been lost were it not for his safety harness. It became apparent that something was wrong. The jib-top wouldn't come down. The halyard was loose, and the wind pulled at it harder than we ever could, but still it stayed up. It was caught at the head of the mast. Yet it had to come down. The downhaul was taken and wrapped around the anchor windlass, the strongest winch on the boat. It was started, and the strain was immediately apparent. Even before, the line had so much tension on it as to make it as hard as oak. It wasn't a flexible piece of rope, but a solid thing like a pipe that would hurt if you bumped against it. You could step on it, and it would barely flex. And that was during normal sailing conditions. Now it was strained beyond that. The windlass which easily pulled our two-hundred-fifty pound anchor and three-hundred feet of chain out of the mud could not free that jib. The fight was tremendous, and in the end neither side won but the line broke. It burst like a bullet ripping through flesh, like a train crash, and a heart attack. It didn't unwind slowly and suspenseful, like in the movies, but ex-ploded with violent terror. The highest sail on the boat was now secured with only its sheet, and the downhaul thrashed about wildly like a nylon whip.

My heart pounded and my mind raced at all the sights and sounds around me; the scathing winds, the pounding seas, the downhaul whipping around in a demented pattern, cracking loudly, as if the boat was a crazed cowboy and we were helpless cattle, and the tension on my safety harness keeping me this side of alive. It's a storm at sea, and there is nothing else. No tomorrow, no yesterday, no hometown, no anything. It is a vortex, a black hole into which everything you've ever known or thought you could count on is lost as meaningless, and crashes into itself leaving you with nothing but your immediate reality, right here, right now.

So it was with great surprise that I saw the captain standing on the foredeck as if he were at poolside. He had one hand in his pocket and the other holding onto the main staysail halyard. "Someone's got to go up and free that jib-top," he said quite simply. A lifetime at sea had inured him to such situations. My watch mates and I eyed each other uncomfortably. Apparently, it also instilled in him a strange sense of humor. He looked at me, "You do it, Chris. You like to climb." And he walked back into the pilot house. His orders were not to be questioned. My feet knew this and they brought me to the base of the main mast. My head wasn't quite so sure, I hesitantly started up the foot holds thinking, "What the hell am I doing?" I neared the first spreader, looking only at each step in front of me. The wind was blowing through the rigging so fast as to make it whistle and even scream like the tires of a car screeching to a halt. I reached the second speader, and squeezed my eyes shut against the burning salt-water spray. The next rung was in my hand, and I pulled myself up to it. To pull ones self up, so natural yet so contrary to nature. Defying gravity, the pull of the earth and earthly decay itself, climbing away from the very soil we are destined to. At the third spreader, as far as I had gone last time, I stopped and looked around. The boat rocked, and the bow smashed through wave after wave like a broomstick through windows. We were crashing and forcing our way forward, plowing a wide fallow furrow of water. I was primal man, out of breath, prehistoric and dumb, climbing up rung by rung. It was an evolutionary ladder, man, and I climbed it until my arms and legs burned and the salt of my sweat mixed with the saltwater blowing in the air. I was aloft on a cold rainy night, burning with heat from within, as the cold air pounded me from with-out. I was hot in a cold world as I made it past the fourth spreader and all the way to the very top of the main mast. I opened my mouth and screamed a great scream that was muted by the noise of the storm. Cold air rushed into lungs. I thrust it back out, louder and stronger, warm and alive. I was at the top of a mast that heeled almost forty five degrees, and was hanging with just my hands and feet, directly over the water, with nothing to break my fall but the apathetic briny deep.

I held onto the steel forestay with my right hand and the port shroud with my left, as if at the peak of a great pyramid. I moved to get my safety harness hooked to something before I did what I had to do. The cold was caustic. The wind, the spray, and the forestay all cut through my skin. I reached out with the clip of my harness, holding on with just one hand, but it was too much, too much... My fingers began to tremble then my whole arm, it spread to my legs, and finally my whole body shook terribly, as I was perched there with my harness two inches away from being latched on. I didn't know what to do. It was painfully slow the way I started to slip. I was a pitiful sight, as I looked at the masthead light longingly with great sorrow and disappointment. It was a big shining diamond I almost had but was loosing, as I began uncontrollably inching downward, shaking and cowering like a scared puppy until I just couldn't hold on any longer. I lost my grip, and screamed as I saw the shining white masthead light falling, falling away from me. Then, from above, I saw that it was me that was falling. Gaping, I watched me fall, fall, then disappear under the surface of the water in a distant silent splash. In slow motion, I surfaced as the boat continued on at twelve and a half knots, but they weren't stopping! Why weren't they stopping? Hadn't they seen me fall? Wait! Wait! Three minutes, and they're half a mile away. It can't be, they're going on without me! Forgetting me as if I never got aboard. I saw the shining-diamond masthead light get smaller and smaller, as I bobbed on the cold black water. I was being abandoned by my ship.

I was abandoning myself.

I died on that boat, but it was only a part of me that died. The part that didn't want to come on that trip, didn't want to risk losing what it had for what it might get, the part that would rather live in slumber than try to live its dreams. Now the dream was lived; and that part, that voice that dared not risk it, was dead and would be heard no more.

The rest of me that stayed up on the mast hooked on my harness and found that the halyard was caught in the masthead fitting. I took out the knife I brought up and cut through the one-inch line and the sail fell free. It slipped down the forestay into that safe spot in the bowsprit netting, and was tied up like a mummy by the rest of the crew.

I stayed aloft, exalted in my insignificance, for quite a long time. The boat heeled over a comfortable thirty degrees now, and on the leeward side I was still over the water. Nothing protected my fall, but nothing had to. I wasn't going to let go.

I let myself down slowly to the deck. "Well done," the captain said, and my mates seemed to agree. I was initiated and was one of them now.

The wind still rushed and the sea churned; but the boat sailed steadier, even-keeled and smooth as the sun rose off our port quarter.

TWENTY THREE

May 10, 1992
1:30 PM

The storm lasted until the early afternoon, then settled down to a steady breeze. (That night at 12:00 the note, "284 miles in twenty-four hours!" was written in the log book.) We again set all the sails, including the jib-top (after the boatswain went up the mast in nicer weather to splice a new fitting to the end of the halyard), and didn't once change them or even tack for the rest of the way to Newport. My mates had never been to the United States, and were worried they wouldn't fit in. They knew about it only from t.v, and thought car chases were an everyday occurrence. They looked at me as some sort of typical American, and turned to me for guidance.

I should say that when not on duty, eating or sleeping, I was either exploring somehow, such as climbing in the rigging (by the time we got there I had callouses to be proud of), or peering over the side in search of bottles with messages. Or searching for glimpses of my far off place just over the horizon, or else I was reading my book, Joseph Conrad's *Chance*., (The first time I read it on watch my mates asked where the last twenty pages were. I told them of how, in the police station in Antigua, they didn't have any toilet paper, and the book was an old paperback with relatively soft pages... They thought this was the funniest thing and asked, "Why didn't you use the beginning which you'd already read?" So I had to explain to them why I read Conrad. "I don't care how it ends," I said, "I read Conrad for the texture of his writing, not for his great endings. Just as someone might sail to Newport, not for the sake of arriving in Newport, but for the breath of the sea he breathes on the way. It's the getting there that's important." (Still, I thought it was funny because I imagined one of the dumb thugs at the police station sitting on the can and trying to struggle through the last fifteen pages of that difficult book.)

In contrast the crew spent their off time either watching t.v. or playing video games on the computer. I can understand city people who stick their noses in wine glasses and fill their ears with classical music and their eyes with well-decorated interiors because their natural surroundings have nothing nice smelling, sounding, or looking. But to do so here? They would play a sky-diving video game down below, when above was a 143-foot mast reaching into a real life sky. They would watch video taped reruns of "The Dukes of Hazard," when their own lives were potentially so much more exciting. They would let other people live their lives for them on t.v. and in the movies, while they sat on their asses munching chips. But then, that's what most Americans do. "Don't worry fellas," I said, "you'll fit right in."

Such potential for great beauty today, yet we spend our

days in mundane drudgery. A life is the sum total of all its moments and to waste even one is a sacrilege. And to start spending them well is immediately rewarding. We can see the surface of other planets and into the mysteries of atoms, yet we sit on the couch glossy-eyed watching bad sitcoms and tabloid news shows like a passenger in a car watches the scenery go by on the way to their own funeral. It's a nation-wide procession on couches and soft chairs. We're ripping ourselves off of our own precious moments. We're looting our own lives of their substance by the simple sin of omission. We're leaving out our life so that we can do...nothing. Better to make your own life worth watching, than to watch shallow, empty, make-believe lives from somewhere else. Use your imagination. You have the real thing right in your hands. Better to do nothing at all, to spend some moments in still silence, then to waste them mindlessly. All reality guarantees us is the succession of moments, and with them the succession of opportunities; but once they're gone, they're gone. It's one less chance, one less opportunity to add to your life. Destiny calls in small whispers, not obvious shouts. But if you get into the habit of ignoring them, they may stop all together. If you don't answer the phone, April may hang up. April calls but she might not keep calling. As long as we are alive, it is not too late to start listening, but why wait?

Also, the deep conversations I had hoped for never materialized. Maybe, if there were only three of us on watch, it could've been different. Two people can confide in each other, three can discuss, but there is no wisdom in four or more. From four up the possibility of intelligent discourse seems to diminish proportionately. They told crude jokes, and talked mainly about sex. I could've talked their ears off about sex, but I didn't. As shallow as it may seem, when sex with someone is really good, it makes it easier to overlook other things. Two weeks previous I was in a relationship glued together with good sex. Not rapture, nothing beyond time and space, no out-of-body experiences, just good sex and lots of it. Autumn and I may not have always had much to say to each other, but we always liked to make love. You can grow attached to a person that way, emotionally I mean. Autumn and I did, which is what made it so hard to leave.

Contrarily, my mates had been on this boat for years, traveling from port to port, and it was a regular topic -if not a distant mystery for them. When we were in the Bermuda triangle, the Australian said, "Last time I was in the Bermuda triangle I had a wank (masturbated), and impregnated a whole planet of cat-eyed women in the fourth dimension. My dick was in a circle of light from my port hole window, and the stuff just came out and disappeared. Poof! Two months later I'm the proud papa of thirty million screamin' cat-eyed babies."

I went off to check the sail trim, and ended up standing on the foredeck with my eyes on the horizon.

Being at sea is like being at sea. It is everything and nothing. It can be the most exhilarating and most boring thing a person can do. The metaphors of it run deeper than our ability to understand them, yet at times they can seem like shallow cliches. It is nothing like a mountain top. It shares no qualities with a Kansas cornfield. Other things are like it, but it is like no other thing. It is the ever constant, afloat on the ever changing.

It is an earthquake all day and night.

I've been in two earthquakes, including the one in California on October 17, 1989. I was walking down the street in Monterey and the ground rolled and shook for about thirty seconds, windows rattled, there was the sound of breaking glass. It was far less motion than one would feel on a small sailboat, even inside the bay. It was much like trying to walk on a moving train. I found it inspiriting, interesting, and over too soon. It wasn't until later that I saw people whom it scared to death.

Other than being in a building that's falling down, earthquakes aren't all that scary or dangerous. It's the idea of what's happening that scares people so much. The thought that the one thing they thought they could count on, that the earth was solid, suddenly can't be counted on any more. The earth becomes for a moment what the sea always is: fluid and changing. Fear in an earthquake is most often not a fear of getting hurt. It is the deep-seated fear of change. And the fear of change pervades all of some peoples lives.

Observe the vacationer who travels thousands of miles (sitting in a car or on a plane where even motion becomes stillness), just to stay in a Holiday Inn and eat at a Denny's exactly like the Holiday Inn and Denny's where they come from. Why even travel, then? And if they see anything too out of the ordinary or meet people too different from them, they have a bad time. ("France was great except for all those greasy French people. At least they had a McDonald's, and Euro Disney was worth looking at.") But it is the subtraction of the familiar, it is the not-ordinary, that makes travel worthwhile, that shows us new things and possibilities, and jolts open the doors to new ideas, thoughts, and ways of understanding.

Where is the great accomplishment in liking and appreciating people and things just like you and just like you're used to? We belong to the exclusive club of the industrial world, unique only in how similar it all is. But exclusive means exclusion, and exclusion generates misunderstanding. Cultural reclusion breeds polarization, and polarization breeds violence. We need to be able to get along with and appreciate people different than us thereby preventing such incidents as happened to me in Antigua, and far worse, to Rodney King in Los Angeles. It is the change, the differentness that should be valued, investigated, and found worthy or wanting. Even Henry Thoreau, who's so famous for not going anywhere for two years, filled much of his book with observations on how Walden Pond changed, not stayed the same.

The watch ended at 2:00 PM, and we went down below for a lunch of hamburgers and french fries, after which I went to my bunk to try to sleep. So often, especially during the late night watches, I'd find myself dozing and wanting nothing more than to sleep. It would be the hardest thing in the dark pilot house just to keep my eyes open. Then I'd get off watch, get in my berth, and I wouldn't be able to close them and would end up reading or writing. This afternoon that wasn't the case. I had a good long nap, and awoke just in time for dinner: beef pot-pies and mashed potatoes.

TWENTY FOUR

May 17, 1992
5:00 PM

The first land we saw on radar was Montauk Point on the tip of Long Island, but the first land visible to the eye was Block Island, ten miles off the east coast of the U.S. I had seen the other side of it from the Rhode Island beach every summer when I was growing up, and this side didn't look much different. The Newport toll bridge came into sight soon after that, and we sailed all the way into Narragansett Bay looking at it, and didn't start our engines until we were almost directly beneath it. The sails started to come down like garments from a woman and soon the masts were naked. The captain was now at the helm with the most serious expression I had seen on him yet. His hands were on the five-foot diameter red cedar wheel and his eyes were all over the perimeters of the boat. The pilot house, which was our living room for this whole trip, was now off limits to the whole crew but him. He scrutinized all the conditions that might effect the boat -the surge, the wind, the other boats, our speed, the nearing dock- and brought the many ton vessel to a gentle halt eight inches away from the dock, as casually as one would put a library book back on the shelf. There were half a dozen people there to meet us, all just because we were a notable boat. They were onlookers who were thrilled to be thrown our dock lines. A man in a suit came up to the captain and introduced himself officiously. He was a member of the local yacht club, extending their welcome to the captain. I had driven over the bridge before, but had never actually been into Newport itself. Now I was arriving like a celebrity. If you plan on going there, I highly recommend arriving on a multi-million dollar sailboat.

After dinner and a check by customs we were allowed into town. It was dark by this time and since it was only the middle May, tourist season hadn't begun yet. The town was slow and semi-vacant. It had that worn-out, well-moneyed east coast tourist town look, like Mystic, Connecticut, Provincetown, or Martha's Vinyard. But it wasn't so bad, since there weren't too many people around.

The crew wandered around in small groups for a while, but all ended up at a collegiate kind of bar with loud music and a pool table. It was half full of Ivy League-looking guys and that summer-in-Newport kind of girl. Tan, thin noses and nice cars, highlighted hair and straight teeth. They spend their days either on the beach in one-piece bathing suits, or cruising around the bay on Boston Whalers wearing white college sweatshirts. Their nights are spent in little groups at tables in the bars, with their legs crossed once at the thigh, tilting glasses to their mouths while their heads stay still and their eyes scan around the room. It quickly came up in conversation that yes, we were off the boat that just came in, followed by questions about the boat, island life, ocean sailing, etc. Someone bought us a pitcher of that great symbol of American bad-taste Budweiser beer, and I sipped a glass, missing the best beers in the world, brewed right in the Seattle area. I wondered how I'd get back there. That was definitely what I wanted to do. I was to be off the boat in the morning. That didn't bother me. I had two dollars and a one-way plane ticket from Antigua to San Juan, Puerto Rico. That was a little more disconcerting. I figured I could do three things. One, hitchhike all the way out west. That was not appealing. Two, hitchhike back to my hometown in Connecticut to mooch off and borrow money from old friends who I haven't kept in touch with, and now have nothing in common with. That was even less appealing. Three, get a ride to the airport in the morning with the crew who were going in a rental car to pick up the first mate, and somehow convince American Airlines to bring me back to Seattle. I reckoned that if three didn't work I could always fall back on one and two, so it was easily settled.

Since its early days, Newport has been descended upon by rowdy boat crews just back from sea, but we weren't one of them. We were all back to the boat by midnight, and I was asleep by one.

In the morning, it was breakfast as usual. After breakfast, all the deckhands were put to scrubbing the decks, and I packed up my small bag and got ready to go to the airport with the stewardess and the engineer. I shook hands with the captain in sincere thanks. "It's been a pleasure having you aboard," he said with a nod. I deboarded for the last time and waved to my old mates, who waved back disheartenedly with sudsy sponges.

Once at Boston's Logan airport I said, "See ya'" to the cook and engineer and was off on my own again with just my pack on my shoulder and my sneakers on the ground. I jogged to an American Airlines ticketing line, and when it was my turn, I said to the young woman behind the counter with all the seriousness I could muster, "I need to speak to a supervisor." I felt like Hunter S. Thompson trying to sneak into a cop convention as I tried to persuade the supervisor to get me on a $473.00 cross-country flight with a $233.00 inter-island ticket. She said it wasn't their responsibility to make sure their passengers have return tickets. She said it wasn't her fault or her problem that I lost all my money in a casino. She didn't care that I got so hassled by immigrations. It was no concern of her's that I was now going to miss the Olympics and Worlds Fair. But when I got to the part about the American Airlines ticketing woman in Antigua saying, "Get the fuck off our island, boy," and a slight exaggeration about my father being a corporate lawyer, she quickly found me space on a flight leaving in half an hour.

This was on the morning of May 18th. As I settled back and the plane taxied to the runway, I felt a keen sense of accomplishment for having dealt with her so well. "I really got what I wanted," I thought. Then I looked at my tickets.

A twelve-hour lay-over in Chicago? A nine-hour lay-over in Denver? She too had gotten what she wanted; I was out of her hair. As the plane blasted down the runway and took off I felt like shaking my fist out the window and yelling facetiously, "You'll hear from my Dad!"

First thing I did in Chicago was try to change my ticket

but, of course, everything was booked. We had been given snacks on the plane from Boston, so when I sat down to a twelve-hour wait in Chicago I had in my pocket five little bags of peanuts, a biscuit I had pilfered from breakfast on the boat, and exactly two dollars. I imagined sitting in that seat for twelve hours meditating like a Tibetan monk and achieving some transcendental airport-wait state, but it didn't go anywhere. My stomach grumbled and two obese women beside me started talking about what good deals they got on their new weight loss programs. "I signed up for just $450.00," one said as her double chin jiggled, "and it really seems to be working." My stomach growled loudly as if antagonized. I lost twelve pounds on that trip. From 190 pounds to 178. I would've gladly sold them my "total life disruption" weight loss program for a mere $425.00. Instead, I put a salted peanut in my mouth and chewed it slowly.

TWENTY FIVE

May 18, 1992
All Day

There's a reason nothing really exciting ever happens in airports. It's because when you're in them you are nowhere. You're not where you're from, you're not where you're going. You're in that indescribable interim in between, in the capitol of the modern province, "Noplace." I literally could not distinguish between Chicago and Denver. The people had no distinguishable features, the air was without scent, the climate controlled, the music piped in. The quality of sunlight is noticeably different in high altitudes than low altitudes, in dry climates verses humid ones, in the east and the west, but you can't tell that through tinted windows. If I wanted the world to be rose-colored, I'd have worn sunglasses. A place is a quality of light, of air, sounds and smells, a certain feel, as much as it's a set of coordinates on a map. I was experiencing the enormously strange accomplishment of the western world: the ability to not be where you are.

From airports to shopping malls to condominium developments to the best colleges of the east situated right in the east's worst slums. With what connection we have to where we actually are, we may as well live on the moon. Going to the moon was as much a statement of how completely we can isolate ourselves from our surrounding as it was a scientific quest. It was an exercise in modern living. The airport I was in was a sapling moon station. And in the same way that I wasn't really in Chicago or Denver, no one has ever really been to the moon. Neil Armstrong walked on shoes made in Detroit, breathed Florida air, and ate food from Nebraska. His ship shouldn't have said Apollo on it, it should've said Winnebego. It was the most costly mobile home/recreational vehicle ever built, and brought us back as useful a perspective of our world as one gets of our country through the window of a Greyhound bus doing 65 down highway 90. That is, a useless one.

There is a way of thinking called "train of thought." There was an intellectual movement called "stream of conscious-ness." Today, for the "space age" we have a corresponding metaphor: the person we call "spacey." The Random House Webster's College Dictionary defines "space cadet" as "A person who seems dazed or out of touch with reality due or as if due to drugs." What does that say about our culture? It says that we are like astronauts -passengers in a world we did not create and can barely understand.

I already wasn't enjoying my day-long stay in the airport, when a very old man occupied the seat beside me. It would've been better had he not started talking. We were both silent for a while before he said, "I never been on a plane before. Been on a train during World War One, 1917, but that was different." He continued though I didn't reply. "That flying is just too expensive as far as I'm concerned."

"Where ya' headed?" I asked.

"Out west. My daughter's flying me out there. I wouldn't waste the money on it myself."

"Too expensive?" I said.

"That's right." There was a long pause as if he was rolling a cigarette, though he wasn't; then he continued. "I mean I only have $336,000 dollars in the bank. Start wasting money like that, next thing you know you're down to nothing," and he repeated to himself, "Down to nothing."

My jaw dropped. "How old are you," I asked.

"Ninety-three," he said. "It's easy for me to figure because I was born in 1899 so I'm always just one more than the year."

"And you have $300,000 dollars, in the bank?"

"A bit more. But it's not as much as it used to be, you know. Just yesterday I read about a heart operation that cost $450,000. What if I need one of those."

"Your insurance will cover it."

"You can never be sure, you know. I could end up broke."

I felt like I was sitting next to my antithesis, next to a man who lived his life in the exact opposite manner I had so far. So, I asked him, "What were you doing when you were twenty five?"

"Twenty five? Lets see that was..."

"1924"

"Yes, I was back from the war then, married, no kids yet, but I was working. Yes-sir-ee, working and saving. Gotta save, you know. Right after the war I got a job stocking shelves in a stationery store. Worked my way up to manager by the time I retired. Fifty two years, never missed a day. Yep," he said, "stationery was my life."

That took a minute to sink in. "First time west?" I asked.

"First time out of Chicago since the war."

Zen teachings say we should try to be like water which is content with and conforms to its surroundings without complaint. If it's cold it freezes, if it's hot it evaporates, put it in a glass and it conforms to the shape without complaint. But is it so hard to imagine water preferring some states to others? A clear blue stream to a mud puddle? A mountain snowflake to city slush? The warm blood of a dolphin darting through waves in the South Pacific to a warm can of Coke forgotten in a broken refrigerator in an abandoned gas station near Hoboken, New Jersey? We are mostly water. Is it so hard to say "I'd rather be clinging tenaciously like an icicle to a mountain side in Alaska, than sitting on a counter at home like a glass of water regardless if it's half full or half empty? It's not the conformation to our surroundings we should strive for, but the alteration of them to something we value. Water may or may not be able to do this, but we certainly can.

This man was born in the age of the horse and carriage and lived through the beginning of cars, planes, jets, even space flight and moon landings, and he did nothing but conform like a drudge! Maybe I had no right to, but still I felt enraged. I've met world travelers who, in their search for the interesting become themselves totally uninteresting. Like t.v. watchers who spend their whole lives in search of something new and exciting, and in the meantime become old and boring. But this guy wasn't like that. He didn't even try. Life to him was something to be saved and stored away for the "just in case." Until the "just in case" comes and it's your funeral, and thank God you have enough to pay for it. He was the ideal employee, never missed a day of work in his life, never lived a day of his life either.

I wanted to grab him by the lapels and shake him, yelling, "Live, live, live now while you still have the chance! Drink some wine, fall in love, do something, be something other than just a mindless saving machine! You can't put your life in the bank. You think you're gaining interest, but when you go to withdraw it you find it stolen by time. Either you splurge on a round-the-world cruise at the age of ninety-three, when you can't even get an erection and you meet beautiful women only to have them spoon-feed you your geritol, or else you end up on your death bed not wanting to splurge on fresh-squeezed orange juice. Afraid to live for ninety years, and at the end of them afraid to die. But as long as you're here, it's not too late. As long as you're here it's not too late!"

I felt like saying, "All the money you have is in direct proportion to how much you have not lived! Get in the habit of storing your life away and you find it gone. Get in the habit of living your life with passion and you can do it even if you're broke. Everyone dies, but not everyone lives." I felt like saying a lot of things. Out of a respect for elders I said nothing. I thought to myself, "I want to die in debt."

He spoke up again. "You know, now that I think about it I got kind of sick on that train ride. I wonder where I could find some motion sickness medicine in this place."

I told him I had some, and before I knew it I was mistakenly holding out to him an unopened box of condoms. "Won't be needing those," I thought, as the young stewardess sitting across from us nervously looked away. I switched boxes and gave him two pills.

The latex condom, I thought, perfect symbol of modern love and modern life. A life when no one touches anything any more. Not their food, not the ground, not even their lovers. There is an "ultra thin" barrier between us and the real world. Like man on the moon. Space suits were just full body condoms for the great Space Fuck. They were the one-man prototype of what so many people call home today. Why do you think they call them "condominiums?" But, as I sat next to this man, I thought that even if adventurous and exciting lives must be somewhat contrived today, it is better than no adventure at all. It's like sex with a condom; maybe it's not quite the real thing, but it's far better than no sex at all. Living a pure life in this modern world is like two virgins making love; the opportunity is rare. But my whole point is that while we may live in a prefabricated world, it is still possible to live a full life. And even if adventure is contrived and the real thing often separated from us slightly, there are still great things to do. And doing anything is far better than doing nothing at all. The day when a frontier engaging all the senses was a common possibility may not be here any longer, but that only means that if you want such an experience you must do uncommon things.

When I finally got on my plane for Seattle I was incredibly hungry, and was seated next to a skinny fifteen-year-old dressed in a leather jacket, black t-shirt and torn jeans. His long hair was pulled back in a pony tail. He was the opinionless teenage rebel of today. One who believes only that you can have no beliefs, whose only icons are iconoclasts, and who values only not value-ing. But he had the redeeming quality of a bag lunch his mother gave him as he got on the plane.

"What did mom make you?" I asked, with hungry eyes shifting from my magazine to the bag.

"Peanut butter and jelly, two Twinkies and an orange. Except I hate oranges. Do you want it?"

It was the tastiest orange I ever had.

On this flight I was again given peanuts and a drink. It wasn't long before we leveled off at thirty thousand feet and I fell asleep. I had a dream of oranges falling from the sky and landing in the midnight stillness of a small pond. I felt the ripples around me, bouncing off my shores, and meshing like a woven basket, then holding only a mirror of the previous stillness.

TWENTY SIX

May 19, 1992
10:30 AM

I stepped off the plane into a sunny Seattle morning and walked to the bus stop in front of the airport. The bus to downtown would've cost $1.10. To get to Port Townsend from there I would've had to take a $3.30 ferry and two more dollars worth of busses. The two crumpled George Washingtons in my pocket shrugged and said, "We wish we could help." But I was comforted by the fact that where I wanted to be was now connected to me by a manageable amount of land. I walked out to the road leaving the airport, enjoying the stretch of my legs and fresh air, and put out my thumb towards Tacoma. I got a ride almost immediately. "I saw you on the plane," he said, and asked, "Where are you coming from?" He got an ear-full.

Things were looking good. He dropped me off in Tacoma where I soon got another ride in a pick-up truck to the small fishing and farming suburb of Gig Harbor. If it keeps up like this, I thought, I'll be back in no time. It didn't.

I stood in Gig Harbor facing south into the mid-day sun for

hour after hour watching car after car go by. I was getting frustrated, hungry and sunburned. The first day I was on Antigua I slept. The next day when I left it was cloudy. The trip was all partly cloudy until I got to the airport in Boston. So, despite the fact that I had been to a tropical island and had been at sea for two weeks, I wasn't very tan. By the middle of the afternoon I could feel the heat beneath my eyes. I was licking my quickly chapping lips and sighing heavily. I went into a convenience store and did something I hadn't done in more than two weeks. I bought something. I bought an apple, a buttered hard roll, and a twenty five cent cup of coffee which I filled one quarter with coffee and the rest with milk and extra sugar figuring it constituted a pretty good meal in itself. The two George Washingtons took deep breaths as if they had been suffocating and said to each other, "I thought we'd never get out of that place!" as they were handed into the cash register. I was given seventy nine cents in change. I got a refill of milky sweet coffee and went back to the curb.

The sun that pounded me at noon was now just below the trees, and I stood in welcome shade. Eventually, a car stopped, and a succession of rides ended with me getting out of a used Volvo at the top of the hill overlooking the most beautiful place on earth, Home; Port Townsend, Washington. The wind was rushing across the bay frothing the water and sending sailboats speeding back and forth like playing dolphins. The sun was shining on billowy cumulus clouds in the distance, making their tops white and shiny like sails and their flat bottoms grey and wet looking. It was as if they, too, were boats sailing the great seas of the sky on magnificent journeys to far away places as I walked down the hill home.

I felt like a stranger as I looked down at the town I had felt so welcome in just a few weeks ago. I was returning a different person. I was broke, jobless, homeless. I could very well be going back to burned bridges and lost friendships, but none of that mattered. I was going to build, to rebuild, to create my life. I was a new person, and I was prepared to start over again from scratch, all alone. I was excited about the challenges, even hardships facing me. I carried my shoulders high the last mile into town not knowing what I was going to do. My apartment had probably been rented and my job filled. I had nothing but my wits, acquaintances, and my small pack. My steps were quick and resolved. I was prepared to spend my last seventy-nine cents on fishhooks and line, and camp out on the outskirts of town and living on blackberries, river trout and rainwater if that's what I had to do to get myself reestablished.

Downtown was strangely silent when I got to it, echoy and dream-like. My old apartment was my first stop. The door was locked. I pictured three possible scenes behind it. One was that Autumn had flipped out and wrecked the place, leaving me with broken furniture, holes in the walls and a huge repair bill. Two was that it was empty and antiseptic, ready for a new tenant. "You just left all that stuff here," my landlady would say, "so I gave it to the Goodwill." Three was that I'd open the door to a bunch of someone else's stuff arranged in a nice homey fashion; a home in which I was not welcome. I tried my key in the lock and it turned.

That was a good sign. There was a fourth possibility I had not considered. My stuff was still there. Autumn had left as she said she would, and there was now just one lonely pillow on the bed, but the place was as bright and sunny as ever. I put my pack down inside. The same pack I had seen beside me for so many hours, I now stuffed deep beneath my bed.

Three weeks is a long time to be unsure. It is a long time to be dead. It's a long time to be a twenty-five-year-old newborn. But it's not a long time for a landlady. I went to her apartment. She was glad to see me but had some bad news. "I didn't know you were coming back so I rented your apartment as of the first of June. You can stay the rest of this month on your deposit, but you have to be out after that."

I felt like shouting, "Twelve days free rent!" but instead I said I thought that would be O.K. I went back to my apartment smiling. Hunger wasn't so bad, I thought, if you have a warm bed to sleep in.

At five thirty I walked to work to pay them a surprise visit. I arrived at the back door of the restaurant to find the part-time pizza maker who was now full-time since I left, and hadn't had a day off in three weeks, smoking and looking worn out even though his shift was just begining. He took one look at me and said, "Welcome back. Want to work for me tonight?" Work meant one thing to me: a free meal. I feigned a moments consideration and said, "Sure, if it's O.K. with the boss." She nodded her approval, and he was out the door running.

It was a slow night of work, but that was fine with me. I would've worked all night just for a sandwich. The boss and I had a talk after work. Not only was it O.K. that I was back, but she said it was crucial. They were quite distressed by my leaving, she said, and really needed my help this summer. She said if I agreed to work the whole summer, she would give me a five hundred dollar advance on my pay. I very nearly turned into a blubbering idiot. "F-f-f-fi-fi-five hundred d-d-d-dollars?" But I kept my cool and accepted her offer with thanks. Work ended with the familiar routine, including going next door to the Uptown Pub for a beer.

Everywhere I looked were familiar faces glad to see me. "Welcome backs" and handshakes abounded. "You really got a lot of sun down there, didn't you," they said. I didn't have the heart to tell them it was a Gig Harbor not English Harbour tan. I felt in a similar shock as when I lost all my money, except this time it was shockingly good. It was so hard to believe that at times I felt like reaching out and touching people just to be sure they were real. I felt like saying to one friend, "Your beard looks really good," and rubbing my hand against it as if it were my own. I touched a woman's bare shoulder in what she took as a casual gesture, but what was to me an experience full of meaning and tactile significance.

I was welcomed back heartily, and the glow that was in my face was not as much from the excellent Washington microbrews we were drinking as it was from my incredible good fortune. I was at a table of friends in a friendly local tavern. It was truly amazing, and I wanted to embrace it all in gracious thanks. I raised my glass and said with an irony only I understood, "To the sea!" and the glasses crashed together with a splash and a resounding echo, "To the sea!"

Just then four middle-aged men in crisp Eddie Bauer clothes, obviously from somewhere else, came sauntering in like old salts and sat at the table next to us. One said, with robust pride, "We just sailed here from Shilshole Marina. Are you web-footed enough to know where that is?"

I said as I sipped my beer, "Last week I was sailing in the Sargasso Sea. Do you know where that is?"

TWENTY SEVEN

May 19, 1992
11:30 PM

There's no such thing as a happy ending.

I went home and laid down on my bed with Conrad's *Chance* beside me. That book had no ending, neither happy nor sad, and I thought it fitting. In real life, stories don't have endings. Prince Charming may save the damsel in distress from the clutches of the evil dragon and ride off with her in his arms, but in the scene after "THE END" she burps in his face and tells him of her two bratty kids from a previous marriage. Happily ever after just isn't a reality. It may seem in the grips of great happiness that it is too good to last, or that some hardships are so dismal as to be everlasting, but that's just the limitedness of our vision. Happiness, like sadness, comes and goes while we continue on. I haven't lived happily ever after yet, but that night I laid in bed still and silent, enjoying the succession of good moments which surrounded me as if they were beautiful music. I turned off the light and got beneath the covers in the soft rectangle of moonlight entering through my window. I began to doze off feeling well-fed, secure and happy to be home. I was drifting away contented and ready to get on with my new life when there was a knock at the door.

"Come in," I said quietly.

"Chris?" I heard her say into the darkness, her voice like the flame of a candle.

I recognized it immediately as April's voice. I heard her step quietly through the living room, then saw her come into my room. She sat on the edge of my bed as I sat up. We hugged. "I heard you were back," she said, "how did it go?"

"Pretty good," I understated. "I got on the St. Christopher."

"Really! That's one of the nicest boats there, and how fitting."

"I thought so," I said, and she asked about the delivery. I told her all about it, from racing the tender in St. Maartin harbor, to climbing the mast in the storm, to waiting in the airports on the way back, and ended by pulling a thick wad of cash from my pocket and paying her back the money she loaned me. She was not a little surprised, nor a little delighted. Again, somehow, I found her hand in mine. I asked, "What about you? I thought you were going to California."

She smiled, and lowered her eyes shyly. Hesitantly, she said, "I wasn't going to California."

"What do you mean?"

"I mean, when I called you only said maybe. I didn't think you were coming. Chris, I came back to be with you."

My ears were deceiving me! "Why didn't you say so in the airport?"

"I wanted to. I wanted to turn my ticket in and go with you, but I couldn't. That morning I decided I had enough of that life for a while. Chris, I want to live somewhere for a change. I want to have a place to come home to and a basket of fruit in the window. I was running home and didn't want to ruin your trip. I know how much you thought about and dreamed about that adventure. It's just that I've been feeling a little less adventurous lately. That morning I saw clearly what I really wanted, and I knew I had to come back here. I thought you might've wanted the same thing, and that's why you didn't want to come. When I saw you in the airport I figured I was wrong, and would just take things from there. I wanted you to have a good trip. I didn't want to burden you with my decision."

I reached out to touch her face. "You weren't wrong," I said.

"I wasn't right," she replied.

"No, you couldn't have been more right. This couldn't have been more right."

"Really?" she asked.

I said, "Had I stayed I would've always felt like I missed out on something and asked myself forever, 'What if, what if?' Had I stayed, Autumn would still be here and that would've been a mess. Had you come back to me like that, inside I would've felt I was stifling you and dragging you back against your will, even if you explained otherwise. Your return would've been a symbol of my draining of your life. This way it is a symbol of us bringing life to each other, of us bringing each other to each other, and crossing paths on the way to the same place."

"We were both headed right here," she said with a smile.

"Right here," I agreed.

My hand was still touching her face. We were bathed in

the soft moonlight glow from my window, and there was suddenly a thick tension in the air. Like in an election when all the votes are in and everyone is waiting on the edges of their seats for the results. Waiting to see if what they've worked for and hoped for all these months will become a reality. We were in the campaign headquarters of the biggest election of our lives and the last ballots were about to be counted. We came together in a kiss of triumph and wonder, and the whole office burst open with shouts and cheers and threw paper in the air and toasted us with overflowing bottles of champagne, yelling "We did it!" as they hugged and yelled and congratulated themselves furiously.

This day, which I started out figuring I'd spend the night sleeping on the beach, cold, alone and hungry, without even enough money for breakfast, I went to bed with a job, an apartment, over $200.00 cash, next to the most beautiful woman in the world. It was all too amazing and I could hardly believe it, as in one warm fluid motion April slipped off her pants and slid beneath the covers beside me. Our kisses and embraces were new and wonderful things like food to a starving man. We savored the first touches of our skin like delicacies, and kissed like teenagers for the first time. We were a warm glow radiating beneath the covers.

Some time later she asked, "Do you have any..."

I reached under my bed into my pack and pulled out a small cardboard box. April looked at me funny and said, "I didn't mean seasick pills." I had the box of Dramamine in my hands. It wasn't what I was looking for.